A Pasta TOUR

We all love the charm of Italy and its cliche of daily life ...
hands waving, chaotic roads, dramatic and theatrical conversation,
interesting bureaucracy, villas, coastal views, history,
fashion, olive oil, wine, gelato, vespa rides
and pasta!

I dedicate this book to my family
and the many pasta meals shared at our tables
in Australia and Italy.

A Pasta Tour

Recipes from across Italy

PIA GAVA

Smith Street Books

CONTENTS

PART TWO
CENTRAL

PART THREE
SOUTH

INTRODUCTION

MY PASTA LIFE

Food is life; pasta is life. Italians live and breathe this sentiment every day, either in part or in full!

Pasta has always been so much more than just a meal. It's a way for me to connect to my childhood, family history and Italy, my family's home country. As a child, every Sunday morning I would awaken to the comforting aroma of sugo (sauce) being made in our kitchen. A clatter of pots and pans together with vibrant Italian conversation between my parents would reach my ears. As in many Italian families, my mother was busy in the kitchen, preparing food for the week, using fresh local ingredients and time-honoured practices to feed us. A ritual of constant stirring, simmering and dipping bread into the luscious sugo to taste it was a weekly tradition that produced enough to use for many dishes throughout the whole week. To this day, it's a smell, taste and eating experience that feels like pure comfort.

In my family kitchen, sugo was the traditional accompaniment for either homemade fresh or dried pasta. So many pasta shapes were paired with this simple sauce – long or short pasta, stuffed pastas filled with ricotta, cheese, vegetables or even slow-roasted meat. Of course, we also ate pasta mixed with other sauces or even simply with olive oil, garlic and sometimes fresh or dried chilli.

Another memorable sauce we would often eat was made using vegetables grown in my father's treasured vegetable garden, which had been preserved in oil (a process called 'sott'olio'). We always had a jar of these vegetables (often zucchini/courgette, eggplant/aubergine or green tomatoes) on the kitchen bench, waiting their turn to be transformed into a meal.

Both my parents would create fresh pasta on our red laminate table that Dad had custom built, complete with a matching red tray. Dad would always make his favourite fresh homemade spaghetti while Mum's handmade pasta menu expanded over the years to include fettuccine, ravioli, agnolotti and even gnocchi, just to list a few. Both of my parents had learned these recipes and techniques from their own parents and other family members, and together they created their own blend of recipes and rituals for our family, which they in turn passed on to me.

Growing up, every special-occasion meal would include pasta, whether it was Easter, Christmas, a wedding or even just when family or friends would visit. Every meal would spotlight that family's traditional pairing of pasta and sugo. Some families would include red capsicum (bell pepper), meat or perhaps chilli or eggplant in their sugo, while others might serve a fresh

Napoletana-style sauce. The more time-consuming filled pastas would be handmade for special occasions, or sometimes just because it was Sunday!

Though I was born and raised in Australia, I've been fortunate enough to travel to Italy many times. It was during my first trip to Italy, when I was 20 years old, that I first noticed the difference between the pasta that was served in Italy and what I was used to eating in Australia. In Italy, every pasta dish heroes the simplicity of each delicious ingredient. Even the tomatoes taste different there – perhaps because they're grown from volcanic soil or maybe because Italians know how to use seasonal ingredients so well.

I visited my family in the Abruzzo region during this trip. The meals were especially grand – huge feasts were prepared to welcome me and my other visiting Australian relatives. This was also the trip that I discovered there's only so much pasta that can be consumed in one day!

I still have some cousins who live in the province of Pescara in the Abruzzo region who I try to visit as often as possible. My husband, Tony, has family that live in the Calabria and Umbria regions. Tony was born in Australia, but when he was only one year old his parents decided to move their family back to Italy. Their family moved between the two countries, calling both Australia and Italy home. This feeling of being caught between two countries is common for many Italian–Australian families, and it is one of the main reasons we try to visit Italy so often, to see our families and to feel connected to the beautiful country and its culture.

Each trip to Italy has offered even more opportunities to uncover our traditional family recipes and to explore new restaurants and regional dishes from across the country. After so many trips together, Tony and I now get to blend our distinct family recipes – with some Australian influences thrown in – to pass on to our family.

When travelling across Italy, we are always determined to stray from the touristy crowds and food scene but that isn't always easy. Pasta dishes are often listed on menus just to attract tourists and are usually served in a way that compromises taste and tradition. My thoughts on being a visitor in Italy are complicated, given I was raised with such a strong link to the culture and our families. Because of this we don't always feel like tourists in Italy, but ultimately we still are. And we now know that any restaurant that charges more than €2.50 for an espresso is definitely a tourist trap!

It has always been rewarding to travel to restaurants that were out of the way, or to seek out small businesses or family-run places that were passionate about sharing their own specialty dishes. Some family restaurants wouldn't even offer a menu, which could feel risky. Instead, they would simply tell us what dishes were on offer that day, often based around what seasonal produce was available. Fortunately, these menu-less gambles have always paid off, and we've enjoyed some very memorable meals over the years.

One of our favourite meals was at a restaurant near a picturesque wharf in Sicily – a small business run by a beautiful husband-and-wife team. They didn't have a menu; instead, they asked what we felt like eating that day. They lovingly cooked with passion, moving around in their kitchen with calm but shared enthusiasm. The pasta we had was served with a light tomato and basil sauce, then dessert was accompanied by an espresso and a small digestivo. While we ate, they chatted with us about our day and gave us tips about other places to eat, all in a relaxed atmosphere, just like we were family.

So much of my connection to Italy continues with my cooking for friends and family, using recipes from my parents, from Tony's family, and from other cooks who inspire me with their creative takes on Italian food and, of course, pasta.

I set out on the adventure of researching this book fuelled by a desire to relive memories of countless pasta meals I have had the pleasure of eating throughout my life, and to better understand why this staple Italian meal is so different across the country. So many questions swirled in my mind: Why are egg-based doughs more common in the north of the country, and water- and semolina-based doughs more common in the south? What towns did iconic shapes like penne, tagliatelle and pappardelle come from? The history of pasta was calling me!

Learning about Italy through the lens of one of the country's staple meals, one that represents the comforts of home, has allowed me to learn more about my family's homeland, the history and traditions which have shaped each dish, and to appreciate the versatility and continued evolution of pasta.

Cuisine is never static; in recent years, modern restaurants have offered inspired pasta dishes, creatively reinventing these dishes or revisiting lost classics with amazing pasta menus. I have noticed that many modern pasta dishes begin with tradition at their core. Even if the combination of flavours is seemingly new and original, there is always a sense of familiarity that reminds you of childhood, of family gathered around a table.

I hope this cookbook entices you to join me on this pasta journey. Together we will travel through Italy's 20 regions, discovering ingredients and flavours that once served noble families, as well as the simple dishes born from necessity. Pasta suits every mood, and together we'll learn how to create each dish by focusing on local ingredients and what is abundant in each region.

Andiamo ... let's go!

TRAVELLING THROUGH MY COOKBOOK

My love for traditional pasta dishes is immense. There are many pasta dishes distinct to each region – in fact, there are over 300 unique pasta shapes and each is matched to a specific sauce! These culinary traditions must be kept, treasured and continued to be handed down; however, there's always room for updated and re-imagined versions of dishes, especially as access to ingredients and cooking methods evolves.

I hope to share and honour the origins and traditions of pasta making in this book with recipes you can still easily create at home. You will notice the differences between the regions as we travel from north to south, but you will also find some overlap in flavours and ingredients, given the shared history of these close neighbours. This is the part I adore because these similarities link each region together, like a culinary puzzle. This cookbook invites you to roam through Italy with a touch of history, geography, culture and, most importantly, an appetite for pasta!

I have chosen a few of my pasta favourites from each region in this book. I hope you enjoy them as much as I do.

Allora, let the pasta travel begin!

TRENTINO-ALTO ADIGE/SÜDTIROL
VALLE D'AOSTA
FRIULI-VENEZIA GIULIA
LOMBARDIA
VENETO
PIEMONTE
NORTH
EMILIA-ROMAGNA
LIGURIA
TOSCANA
MARCHE
CENTRAL
UMBRIA
ABRUZZO
MOLISE
LAZIO
Roma
CAMPANIA
PUGLIA
SARDEGNA
BASILICATA
SOUTH
CALABRIA
SICILIA
ITALY

A TOUCH OF ITALIAN HISTORY

Pasta has always been shaped by the history, politics and geography of Italy. Long before unification, regional cultures, trade routes and systems of governance influenced how grain was grown, which ingredients were available, and how pasta was made, shared and celebrated. These influences have evolved over time, creating the rich tapestry of pasta shapes, sauces and traditions we know today.

The political history and geography of Italy's regions have played a particularly important role in shaping its food. Prior to the unification of Italy in 1861, the country had been divided into several kingdoms and small states, including the Kingdom of Piemonte-Sardegna in the north, the Papal States in Central Italy and the Kingdom of the Two Sicilies in the south. Lombardia-Veneto was under Austrian rule, while San Marino retained its independence. Each region developed its own culinary identity, shaped by local agriculture, cultural exchange and access to resources.

The islands, too, followed distinct historical paths. Sardegna developed its own feudal traditions, while Corsica, originally part of the Papal States and later the Republic of Genoa, was ceded to France in 1768 following decades of conflict. These histories continue to influence the food cultures of both islands today.

Since unification, Italy has experienced an ongoing north–south divide, driven by economic, political and social differences, as well as differences in agriculture and infrastructure. This divide is reflected in pasta itself – in the grains used, the presence or absence of eggs, and the sauces that define regional cooking. Arguably, these distinctions, and the North–South rivalry, are still felt today.

But my pasta tour isn't about reinforcing that divide. Instead, I've organised the regions into three parts – north, central and south – echoing the Italian tricolour flag: green, white and red. These colours symbolise the country's unity and shared identity, linking landscape (green), faith (white) and charity (red), a theme I also explore in My triplo raviolo on page 275, a recipe which is very close to my heart and which finds a way to marry culinary traditions from across this vast country.

I love discovering traditions from many cuisines – there's always history or a story that gives you confidence in a recipe. When you embrace and create a traditional recipe, you become part of the shared story!

And then there's pasta – perhaps the most unifying force of all! I hope this book encourages you to connect with family and friends around a table, sharing stories and traditions over a bowl of delicious pasta.

A TOUCH OF PASTA HISTORY

The origins of pasta are the subject of much debate, with many differing opinions about when, where and how it first appeared in Italy. A popular legend claims that Marco Polo – the renowned Venetian writer, explorer and merchant who travelled extensively through Asia between 1271 and 1295 – brought pasta to Italy in the 13th century. This theory has since been debunked, as pasta existed in Italy long before Marco Polo's time.

Some believe that pasta originated with the Etruscans, a pre-Roman civilisation in Central Italy. Archaeological findings inside an Etruscan tomb include what may have been pasta-making tools, as well as drawings depicting foods that resemble pasta. Called 'testaroli', this pasta is believed to have originated with the Etruscans approximately 2000 years ago. The name is derived from the cooking method, using a testo – a hot, flat cast-iron or terracotta pan. This ancient pasta was made from a simple batter of flour, water and salt, which was poured into the testo in a crêpe-like layer and cooked before being cut into squares, rectangles or diamond shapes. Their texture resembled either a thin sponge (like a crêpe) or thin bread. Testaroli was traditionally served with pesto – linking it to ancient Italian culinary traditions – or simply dressed in olive oil, garlic and either pecorino or parmigiano cheese.

Another theory suggests pasta was introduced by Arab travellers and traders in Sicily between the 8th and 9th centuries. Written records by an Arab geographer document the production and export of dried strands made from durum wheat and water, resembling spaghetti, which were ideal an ideal food for long sea voyages.

While the exact origins of pasta remain unclear, we do know that it was enjoyed in Italy from the medieval period. Our love for pasta has been recorded and depicted over many centuries through literature, artworks and sculptures, such as the painting *Il Mangiamaccheroni* by Mathias Stomer from the 17th century and the book *Il Decameron* by Giovanni Boccaccio from the 14th century. These artworks confirm pasta's longstanding importance and central role in Italian cuisine.

Although pasta is now a staple on the Italian table, it didn't become part of the everyday family meal until the 16th century. Before then, durum wheat was difficult to source in Northern and Central Italy, as it had to be transported from the south. Once durum wheat became more widely accessible, it led to further developments in pasta making across family kitchens, farms, factories and markets. And now, for Italians, pasta is life.

PASTA MUSEUMS

If, like me, you have a passion for pasta history and you're able to travel to Italy, consider adding the following museums to your list of places to visit: the Museo della Pasta in Corte di Giarola (near the city of Parma in Emilia-Romagna), and the Giovanni Fabbri Museum in Chianti, Tuscany, are both well worth a visit!

REGIONAL PASTAS

The differences between northern and southern Italian pasta are vast, and every dish carries its own history. The origins of a pasta dish were always shaped by the availability of produce in the region – whether eggs were used, which type of flour was accessible, as well as whether butter or olive oil was the primary cooking fat. Climate and agriculture also played a big role in determining whether vegetables, meat or seafood were used, and how families decided to create a dish.

In the northern regions, fresh pasta is typically made with eggs and 00 flour (also called grano tenero or doppio zero), an extra-refined soft wheat flour. Gluten does not develop easily unless the dough is well kneaded and rested, resulting in a tender, delicate texture.

In the southern regions, pasta dough was simpler, generally made with just flour and water, but by no means does this make the pasta from these regions inferior. The most commonly used flour is semolina rimacinata, a twice-milled, fine-consistency flour made from ground durum wheat. Slightly yellow in colour, it is often used for hand-rolled shapes such as cavatelli or orecchiette. It has high absorbency and produces an elastic, chewy dough.

In Central Italy, both 00 flour and semolina rimacinata were often combined. This may reflect the overlap between northern and southern traditions, but flour choice also depended on the pasta shape, dish and local customs. The most recognised use of combined flours is found in the region of Emilia-Romagna, in the central–north of the country.

Some regions also added milk and/or oil to their dough, providing richness and flavour and making the dough more supple and easier to shape. White wine can also be added to pasta dough, as the Ligurians traditionally have with their corzetti dough (page 57).

Pasta shapes also determined the sauces they were paired with and how dishes were served. Northern regions relied more heavily on butter and cream as the base for their sauces, while southern regions favoured olive oil, sometimes using it on its own. Simple ingredients have always produced the most flavourful dishes, allowing each component to shine without unnecessary complexity.

RECOGNISING 'TRADITIONAL' PASTA SHAPES AND DISHES

In Italy, several pasta types have received official recognition as 'traditional' food products under the Italian government's Prodotto Agroalimentare Tradizionale (PAT) scheme. This scheme helps preserve long-standing culinary practices, promote regional food identities and recognise foods with a significant history of production.

Some pasta types and dishes that have been recognised under the PAT scheme include:

- **Pizzoccheri** (page 73), a buckwheat pasta from the Valtellina region.
- **Spaghetti alla chitarra** (page 186), a long, fresh egg-based pasta shape from Abruzzo, made by pushing pasta sheets through the strings of a tool called a 'chitarra'.
- **Pasta con le sarde** (page 268), a Sicilian dish made from sardines, raisins, fennel and pine nuts.
- **Agnolotti del plin** (page 42), a variety of pasta ripiena (filled pasta) from the Piedmont region.
- **Bigoli** (page 108), a long variety of pasta from Veneto in Italy's north. Traditionally made in a press called a 'bigolaro', this pasta shape is commonly served in a dish called Bigoli in salsa (page 106).

PRESERVING REGIONAL PRODUCTS AND TRADITIONS

Food products in Italy — and the European Union — are subject to strict labelling regulations designed to protect and preserve regional ingredients and traditional processes from inferior imitations. These protections help prevent food counterfeiting and compromising of quality. Some common protections and designations include:

- **DOP: Denominazione di Origine Protetta (Protected Designation of Origin)**
  This designation applies to products that are produced, processed and prepared in a defined geographical area in accordance with recognised and strictly controlled methods. It is considered the highest standard of protection as it prevents the product from being replicated elsewhere. You are likely familiar with a number of cheeses that are DOP protected, including Parmigiano Reggiano (produced in Emilia-Romagna) and Pecorino Romano (produced only in parts of Lazio, Sardegna and Toscana).

- **STG/TSG: Specialità Tradizionale Garantita (Traditional Speciality Guaranteed)**
  This designation focuses on the traditional production methods rather than geographical origin. It protects products made using traditional recipes, ingredients and techniques that have remained consistent for a minimum of 30 years, ensuring culinary practices are preserved and passed down through generations.

HOW TO MAKE PASTA

✶
Serves
6
✶

This section outlines the basic process for making two of the most common doughs used in this book: an egg-based dough and an eggless, semolina flour-based dough. Some recipes may include additional flours or wet ingredients, but the core stages of the pasta-making process remain the same.

Here, I go through each stage of the process in detail, with the hope that this can be a section you return to again and again as you cook from the recipes in this book.

Basic egg pasta dough
600 g (4 cups) 00 flour
6 whole eggs (about 330 g/ 11½ oz total)
pinch of salt

Basic eggless pasta dough
600 g (1 lb 5 oz) fine semolina flour
300 ml (10 fl oz) water
pinch of salt

RATIOS

The ratio of pasta dough is a delicate balancing act between hydration and flour. You want the dough to be wet enough to come together into a soft, cohesive mass, but not so wet that it becomes difficult to knead. At the same time, there needs to be enough flour to develop the gluten into a smooth, elastic texture, without the dough becoming so dry that it cracks when rolled or shaped.

For egg-based pasta dough the standard ratio is 1 whole egg per 100 g (3½ oz) flour, per person. However, the actual amount of flour needed can vary depending on egg size, flour type and even the weather – yes, the weather! This standard ratio produces a single serving of spaghetti, tagliatelle or other non-filled pasta, and approximately 3–4 tortelli.

For eggless pasta dough, the standard ratio is 2 parts flour to 1 part water. My basic recipe uses fine semolina flour, which is common across many parts of Italy, though some regions use 00 flour or a combination of flours.

The ingredient quantities for both styles of dough in this section have been scaled up to serve six people, but you can easily adjust the quantities up or down as needed.

MIXING

The traditional method of mixing pasta dough is largely the same, whether you're making an egg-based dough or an eggless dough.

Place the flour on a clean work surface or in a bowl and form it into a mound. Make a well in the centre, then add the wet ingredients (depending on the recipe you are following this may be whole eggs, egg yolks, wine, oil, milk, or a combination of these things!) along with the salt.

I tend to place about 80 per cent of the flour on my work surface and keep the remaining flour to the side. This allows me to incorporate extra flour a little at a time if needed, while keeping any unused flour clean. ➥

Using a fork or your fingers, begin slowly mixing the flour into the wet ingredients in a circular motion, adding in flour as needed. This controlled process helps you incorporate only as much flour as needed to form the dough.

At this stage, I sometimes use a dough scraper to cut through the rough dough, ensuring everything is fully combined before I begin kneading.

KNEADING AND RESTING

Kneading is a crucial stage, as it binds the wet ingredients and flour together to create a strong, elastic dough. Using your hands to knead and your fingers to feel for the correct consistency is important. My mum used to say, 'Your fingers will let you know when the pasta dough is done'.

Once the dough has just come together, knead it for about 5 minutes. Use the heel of your hand to push the dough forward and away from you, then fold it back onto itself. Rotate the dough 90 degrees and repeat, kneading until the texture becomes cohesive. If the dough still feels wet while kneading, add a little extra flour and knead for a few more minutes. If it feels dry, lightly wet your hands to add some extra hydration.

Wrap the dough in plastic wrap or place it in an airtight container and rest for at least 20–30 minutes. The dough can be left to rest at room temperature or in the fridge for up to 24 hours. If refrigerated, the dough must be brought back to room temperature before you move on to rolling or shaping your beautiful pasta creations.

Once rested, the dough should be smooth and feel elastic and pliable. Gently press the dough with your finger – it should spring back slightly. If the dough still feels underworked at this stage, you can knead it again for another 1–2 minutes, then rest it for a further 10–15 minutes.

Place the rested dough onto a lightly floured work surface. If needed, you can cut the dough into more manageable portions before shaping or rolling into sheets.

If your pasta needs to be rolled into sheets, continue to the laminating process in the next step. If you're making a shape that doesn't require laminating – such as capunti (page 228), cavatelli (page 205) or orecchiette (page 225) – you can shape the dough at this stage.

LAMINATING DOUGH TO MAKE PASTA SHEETS

Once the dough has rested, it's time to begin rolling it out into pasta sheets (called 'sfoglia'). The sheet-rolling process, known as 'laminating', allows the pasta dough to stretch and strengthen.

You can laminate pasta by hand or, as is more common today, using a pasta machine. I've outlined both methods in this next section.

Laminating with a pasta machine or stand mixer attachment

If you're using a manual pasta machine, make sure it is securely clamped to a clean bench or table.

Working with one of the portions, slightly flatten the dough and guide it once through the widest setting of your pasta machine (depending on your pasta machine, this may be setting 0 or 1 – see note on page 21).

Lightly flour the dough, then tri-fold the pasta sheet by folding one edge over by one-third, then folding the opposite side over the top, as you would fold a letter. Guide the folded pasta sheet through the widest setting of the machine again. If at any point the pasta sheet is getting sticky, you can rub some flour onto the dough before continuing to laminate through the pasta machine.

Tri-fold the pasta sheet once more, then rotate it 90 degrees and roll it through the widest setting again. Repeat this tri-folding and rolling process at least three more times, rotating the dough 90 degrees each time. The tri-folding process helps the dough build strength and structure without tearing, and you'll notice it becoming smoother by the third or fourth pass.

Next, bi-fold the pasta sheet by folding it in half and roll it through the widest setting. Repeat this once more. At this stage, the dough should feel smooth and elastic.

You're now ready to begin rolling out the pasta sheet to your desired thickness. This step allows the dough to gradually stretch further, becoming silky and thin enough to see light shine through.

Adjust the machine to the second-thickest setting and roll the pasta sheet through twice, without folding. Move to the next thinnest setting and repeat. Continue working your way through each setting until you reach the thickness specified in your recipe. A standard thickness for many pasta shapes is 2 mm (approx. 1⁄16 in), about setting 5 or 6, unless otherwise indicated.

Once the dough has reached its desired thickness, you're ready to cut or shape it (page 22). ➥

PASTA MACHINES IN THE HOME KITCHEN

The first manual pasta machine was patented in 1906 by Angelo Vitantonio, and in 1930 Otello Marcato began mass-producing pasta machines under the Marcato brand. These machines were welcomed into home kitchens because they made the pasta-rolling process easier and more consistent.

Further developments followed, including interchangeable roller cutters and, later, motor attachments that enabled faster and less labour-intensive pasta making. I have memories of my mum's motorised pasta machine, which made a high-pitched screeching sound — I'm sure our neighbours also heard it whenever we were creating pasta in our kitchen!

A NOTE ON PASTA MACHINE SETTINGS

It's important to note that pasta machine settings are not universal. Some machines or stand mixer attachments start at setting 0, while others start at 1. For this reason, I've provided the ideal thickness for each recipe in millimetres and inches, along with an estimated range of machine settings to guide you. The exact setting you'll need to roll to will depend on your specific pasta machine.

I use a Marcato Atlas pasta machine, which is one of the most popular brands available worldwide. The table below outlines the approximate pasta sheet thicknesses at each setting and an approximate equivalent for a pasta machine or stand mixer attachment that starts at 1.

As a general rule, if you are using a manual pasta machine that starts with setting 0, work towards the lower end of the suggested range in the recipe; and if you're using a stand mixer attachment or a machine that starts at setting 1, you'll likely need to roll to the higher end of the range.

Pasta sheet thickness guide

Marcato Atlas setting	Stand mixer setting	Pasta sheet thickness (approx.)
0	1	4 mm (approx. ⅛ in)
1	2	3.5 mm (approx. ⅛ in)
2	3	3.2 mm (⅛ in)
3	4	2.8 mm (⅛ in)
4	5	2.5 mm (approx. 1⁄16 in)
5	6	2 mm (approx. 1⁄16 in)
6	7	1.5 mm (1⁄16 in)
7	8	1.3 mm (approx. 1⁄16 in)
8	9	1 mm (approx. 1⁄32 in)
9	10	0.8 mm (1⁄32 in)

Rolling out pasta sheets by hand

Before pasta machines became common, pasta was rolled by hand using a very long rolling pin called a 'mattarello'. Despite the popularity of pasta machines, this method is still widely practised today. I have my mum's mattarello, which was handed down to me, and it will always be treasured. If you don't have a mattarello and wish to roll pasta by hand, you can use a regular rolling pin, though I prefer to use one that's at least as wide as my shoulders, to allow for even pressure to be applied across the pasta sheet. ➥

Place the rested dough onto a lightly floured work surface, knead briefly, then cut into smaller portions. It's best to cover any portions you're not using to prevent them from drying out. Keep a small bowl of flour nearby to dust the dough and work surface as needed. Lightly flour your work surface, then place one portion onto the surface and gently flatten it with your hand or mattarello.

Using the mattarello, begin rolling from the centre of the dough, moving forward and back in slow, even strokes while applying gentle pressure. Roll in this direction a few times until the dough becomes oval in shape, then flip it over and repeat on the other side. Rotate the dough 90 degrees and continue rolling from the centre to encourage even stretching.

Repeat this rolling, flipping and rotating process until the dough has stretched into a large, thin round and you've reached the desired thickness to begin creating your pasta shapes. A good test of readiness is to hold the pasta sheet up to the light – when you can see light through it, the dough is sufficiently laminated and ready for cutting or shaping.

CUTTING AND SHAPING PASTA

At this stage, your laminated pasta sheets or portions of dough are ready to be cut or shaped. The recipes throughout this book provide detailed instructions for making many of Italy's most beloved regional pasta shapes. I've listed some of my favourite shapes on the page opposite, but I encourage you to experiment and discover your own as you cook your way through the book.

COOKING YOUR PASTA

To cook your pasta, bring a large saucepan of water to the boil over high heat, then add cooking salt (1 teaspoon of salt per litre/4 cups of water). The water should be well seasoned, as this is your primary opportunity to add flavour to the pasta.

I like to use a handled colander to transfer the pasta directly into the sauce, so some pasta water will naturally fall into the sauce, along with the pasta. As you toss the pasta through the sauce, you can check if extra pasta water is required. The more you toss, the more the sauce binds, thickens and stabilises.

THE MAGIC OF PASTA WATER

Pasta water is liquid gold! When pasta is cooked in water, it releases starch, which can be helpful to emulsify and bind the pasta with the sauce. This starch acts as the link between fats such as butter and oil and the other liquids in your sauce, preventing separation and creating a stable mixture. It also provides a cohesive, natural thickening and creamy effect, helping sauces cling to pasta without becoming watery.

EGGLESS PASTA SHAPES

- Orecchiette (pictured, page 225)
- Capunti (page 228)
- Strozzapreti (page 123)
- Lagane (page 235)
- Taccozze (page 209)

EGG-BASED PASTA SHAPES

- Tagliatelle (page 125)
- Pappardelle (page 143)
- Tortellini (page 116)
- Fazzoletti (page 69)
- Casoncelli (page 80)

COOK'S NOTES

The recipes in this book use 15 ml tablespoons.

You can, of course, use dried pasta in most of the recipes that include a handmade pasta. This can be a great way to make the recipes in this book even quicker and simpler. Cook the pasta per the packet instructions and add to the sauce for a minute or two before serving.

Some of my recipes call for additional quantities of ingredients like oil, flour, breadcrumbs or cheese 'as needed'. In many instances this will require you to look and taste the dish to see if you think more of that ingredient needs to be added. So much of Italian cooking is intuitive and done by eye — I encourage you to use these recipes be a starting point as you cook from this book!

INGREDIENTS AND TOOLS

INGREDIENTS

Many of the recipes in this book are made using simple ingredients, so the quality of the produce you use really matters.

Flour

Good-quality flour is always in my pantry. Below are some of the most common types you'll find in my recipes:

- **00 flour** Also called 'tipo 00 flour', this is an ultra-fine milled flour made from soft wheat. It is more finely milled than conventional plain (all-purpose) flour and has a moderate amount of protein, which gives the pasta dough its signature elastic, slightly chewy texture, without becoming tough. It is generally used for more delicate pasta shapes such as tagliatelle (page 125) or filled pastas such as tortellini (page 116).

- **Semolina flour** Sometimes labelled as 'semola', semolina flour is milled from hard durum wheat (grano duro). Most dried pasta shapes – such as spaghetti, penne and rigatoni – are made from semolina flour–based doughs, but many hand-made pasta shapes also use this flour, including orecchiette (page 225) and fusilli (page 210). Semolina flour is available in both coarse and finely ground varieties. In my recipes, I generally call for fine semolina flour (also called 'rimacinata').

- **Buckwheat flour** This flour hasn't always been a pantry staple for me, but since researching recipes for this book it has become a favourite! Buckwheat flour is milled from buckwheat seeds; it has a nutty flavour and is naturally gluten free (although it's often mixed with wheat flours for texture, so is not always suitable for people with gluten intolerances). Buckwheat flour is common in northern Italian dishes such as pizzoccheri (page 72).

Eggs

Always use good-quality, free-range eggs in your pasta dough – it's so important. If you're able to buy directly from a local farmer, even better. Trust me, you'll notice the difference.

Recipes in this book mostly call for extra-large eggs, with a cracked weight of approximately 55–58 g (2 oz) each.

Olive oil

Olive oil is liquid gold in an Italian kitchen – whether you're baking, drizzling, frying or simply dipping! I tend to use extra virgin olive oil in my recipes, but occasionally I'll opt for a lighter olive oil when I don't want an overpowering olive oil flavour to come through in the finished dish.

Butter

I use unsalted butter in most of my recipes, which allows me to control the salt content more easily.

Salt

Seasoning is essential when cooking, and salt is a key staple – alongside freshly ground black pepper, of course. I use three types of salt in my kitchen:

- **Cooking salt** A coarse salt that I mostly use for salting pasta water. To salt pasta water, bring a saucepan of water to the boil, then add 1 teaspoon of salt per litre (4 cups) of water.

- **Table salt** Finer than cooking salt and quick to dissolve, this is my go-to salt for everyday cooking and baking.

- **Salt flakes** Light, irregular flakes that deliver bursts of flavour. I like to sprinkle these over dishes just before serving.

Herbs

Whether dried or fresh, herbs are so essential to Italian cooking. I mainly use parsley, basil, sage, oregano and occasionally marjoram in my recipes.

Cheese

A truly essential ingredient. Some regional dishes in this book call for cheeses produced in their region of origin. In many cases these cheeses – such as Parmigiano Reggiano – can only be called by that name if produced in a specific area. Some of my favourite cheeses, which you'll see repeatedly throughout my recipes, include:

- **Parmigiano** Made with cow's milk and aged for a minimum of 12 months. It has a rich, savoury and nutty flavour but can also have hints of sweetness and fruitiness when aged under 18 months.

- **Pecorino** Made with sheep's milk and aged for a minimum of 12 months. It has a bold, sharp, salty flavour and a crumbly texture. Pecorino is ideal for grating or shaving and is used in many classic pasta dishes such as Cacio e pepe (page 172).

- **Asiago** Made with cow's milk, with aging times that vary depending on the style. Pressato (fresh) is aged for around three months; mezzano for up to six months; vecchio for up to 18 months; and stravecchio for longer than 18 months. The fresh version has a mild, creamy flavour, which becomes bolder, sharper and nuttier as it ages.

- **Provola** Made with cow's milk, though some regions also use buffalo milk, this cheese has a mild, sweet flavour and is usually aged for up to four months to retain its sweetness (dolce), or up to 12 months to develop a tangier, saltier flavour (piccante).

- **Ricotta** Usually made from cow's milk whey, though sheep, goat or buffalo milk may also be used depending on the region. Ricotta has a delicate, milky sweetness and a soft texture, making it perfect for filling pasta. A deeper-flavoured variation is ricotta salata, which is aged to produce a firmer, salty cheese that can be grated over dishes.

- **Fontina** A personal favourite. Made with cow's milk and aged for at least three months, Fontina has a semi-soft texture and a mild, creamy, nutty flavour.

Tomatoes

A true Italian kitchen staple! My favourite fresh varieties include vine-ripened tomatoes (I like adding the vines to sauces for a deeper tomato flavour – just be sure to discard them before serving), as well as cherry and roma (plum) tomatoes.

My pantry always contains bottles of passata (pureed tomatoes), tins of polpa (crushed tomatoes) and tinned cherry tomatoes.

TOOLS

My treasured pasta tools originally belonged to my mum, but my own collection continues to grow, with new items constantly joining the pasta party. Many of these tools can be sourced from specialty pasta-making supply stores or online.

Wooden pasta board

I use a large wooden pasta board that is 90 × 60 cm (35½ × 23½ in) as my work surface for pretty much every stage of the pasta-making process. It's ideal for mixing doughs, and the natural texture of the wood gives the dough some resistance when kneading. It's also great when rolling pasta dough into sheets or shaping various pasta forms.

Pasta drying rack or tray

I like to use a mesh drying rack, which allows air to circulate around completed pasta shapes and assists with the drying process.

These racks are useful for drying both long shapes (such as spaghetti or tagliatelle) and smaller shapes (such as fusilli).

Pasta machine and attachments

I use a manual Marcato Atlas pasta machine with several attachments for specific shapes such as bigoli, trenette and fettuccine. I also have my mum's old Imperia machine – and I'm happy to confirm that even after more than 50 years, it still works perfectly.

A popular alternative to traditional pasta machines is using rolling and cutting attachments that fit onto a stand mixer. The majority of stand mixer brands offer a variety of pasta-related attachments, making this a great option if you already own one. Many also offer additional attachments such as meat grinders and even pasta extruders!

Mattarello or rolling pin

A rolling pin will quickly become your best friend. I have quite a few in my collection, but my favourite – and most used – is my mum's mattarello, which you'll catch a glimpse of when I make my chitarra pasta (page 191). A mattarello is a long, thin rolling pin traditionally used for pasta dough.

Round cutters

Perfect for making pasta ripiena (filled pasta) such as casunziei (page 109) or other filled pasta shapes that start from a circle.

Pasta cutters

Similar to small pizza cutters, pasta cutters are great for cutting pasta sheets into uniform shapes. I use both brass and stainless-steel cutters with smooth and fluted edges.

Chitarra

This is one of my favourite pasta tools to use! A chitarra is a wooden frame strung with parallel wires. Pasta sheets are pressed through the strings with a rolling pin, creating square-edged strands.

Pasta knife

This is my go-to tool for hand-cutting long pasta shapes such as tagliatelle (page 125) or pappardelle (page 143). It has a long, straight rectangular blade (generally around 25 cm/10 in long), allowing for even, precise cuts.

Gnocchi board

A small wooden board used to create shapes like cavatelli (page 205) or to add ridges to gnocchi.

Garganelli board

Wider than a gnocchi board, this tool usually comes with a thin rolling pin or wooden dowel. It's perfect for making garganelli (page 135) and also works beautifully for shaping spizzulus (page 251).

Wooden corzetti stamps

These patterned stamps are used to make corzetti (page 57). I have a few different designs and am always looking to add more to my collection.

Potato ricer

An essential tool for mashing potatoes to the perfect consistency for dough for gnocchi or cjarsons (page 98), and key to making passatelli (page 156).

Spätzle tool

This tool intrigued me for a long time. I now love using it to make chnéffléne (page 34) and spätzle tirolesi (page 92). It may seem daunting at first, but trust me – you'll love using it!

Handled colander

I love using a handled colander – it's an easy, mess-free way to transfer cooked pasta directly into a sauce.

TRENTINO-ALTO ADIGE/ SÜDTIROL
FRIULI-VENEZIA GIULIA
VALLE D'AOSTA
Trento
Aosta
LOMBARDIA
VENETO
Milano
Venezia
Alessandria
Parma
EMILIA-ROMAGNA
PIEMONTE
Bologna
LIGURIA
Sanremo

PART ONE

NORTH

Northern Italy is the geographic hat of the country and consists of eight regions. These northern regions share borders with France, Switzerland, Austria and Slovenia. The influences of these neighbouring countries are reflected in the culture, language, history and cuisine. Northern Italian dishes tend to be richer, commonly using butter, cream, potatoes, sausages and cheese. This richness is also reflected in the pasta doughs that are common across this part of Italy. Egg- and egg yolk—based doughs are common in Italy's north, while the flours used range from fine semolina and buckwheat to wholemeal (whole-wheat) and 00, depending on a number of factors, including the specific region's climate, farming practices and traditions.

CHNÉFFLÉNE
(page 35)

PASTA ALLA VALDOSTANA
(page 37)

VALLE D'AOSTA

Valle d'Aosta, or the Aosta Valley, is the smallest region in Italy. The capital, Aosta, is a popular destination for travellers in the winter season, given its proximity to the Alps. The scenery here is spectacular, with high peaks, views of Mont Blanc and world-class skiing. Post-ski, you'll be drawn into the comfort food of this region – heavily influenced by that of its close neighbouring countries, France and Switzerland – the cuisine of Valle d'Aosta is renowned for its dairy, butter and, perhaps most of all, its creamy Fontina cheese.

Dishes in the region are hearty and rich, and include familiar favourites such as gnocchi, polenta, potatoes, risotto, beef and goat stews. Cheese is mainly created from the milk of locally bred Valdostana cattle, but fresh goat's milk is also used. The local Fontina cheese has been produced in the traditional way since the 12th century, usually made from unpasteurised cow's milk.

Pasta isn't really a dominant dish in this region, which makes it a strange place to start in this pasta tour, but the rich and creamy ingredients of the region have made their way into some notable pasta dishes such as lasagne, gnocchi and chnéffléne.

Chnéffléne con cipolle, burro, vino bianco e guanciale

CHNÉFFLÉNE WITH ONIONS, BUTTER, WHITE WINE AND GUANCIALE

*

Serves
4

*

This classic chnéffléne dish uses simple flavours – butter, onion and white wine – paired with delicious, crisp guanciale. I still remember the first time I was served this dish, the sauce was silky smooth and it was pure comfort to devour.

Pasta tools

spätzle-style perforated tool or sturdy metal colander

Pasta

2 eggs (about 110 g/4 oz total)
250 ml (1 cup) full-cream (whole) milk, plus extra as needed
pinch of salt
300 g (2 cups) 00 flour, plus extra as needed

Sauce

200 g (7 oz) guanciale or pancetta, chopped or cut into thin batons
80 g (2¾ oz) unsalted butter
2 onions, quartered and thinly sliced
150 ml (5 fl oz) dry white wine, (such as timorasso, erbaluce or Roero Arneis)
200 ml (7 fl oz) broth (chicken or vegetable)

To serve

grated Parmigiano Reggiano (optional)
small handful of parsley, finely chopped (optional)

For the pasta

Add the eggs, milk and salt to a large bowl and whisk until fully combined.

While whisking, add the flour 100 g (3½ oz) at a time, until a thick batter forms. Set aside to rest for 20–30 minutes. Loosen with a little extra milk if it becomes too thick or add a little more flour if it becomes too thin – we are aiming for a thick, pancake-batter-style consistency.

For the sauce

Meanwhile, heat a large frying pan over medium heat. Add the guanciale and saute for 4–5 minutes, until browned. Remove the guanciale from the pan and set aside.

In the same frying pan, add the butter and onion and saute for 2–3 minutes, until the onion is lightly browned.

Add the wine and cook for another 2 minutes. Season to taste with salt and pepper.

Add the broth and simmer for 5–8 minutes, until the onions soften. Remove from heat and set aside while you cook the chnéffléne.

To cook the chnéffléne

Bring a large saucepan of water to the boil over high heat, then add cooking salt. Working over the boiling water, pour a ladleful of batter into the spätzle-style tool and push/slide it through the holes so the batter drops directly into the water. This will create the 'teardrop' shape. Cook for 2–3 minutes, or until the chnéffléne float to the surface.

Return the frying pan with the sauce to medium heat. Use a handled colander to transfer the cooked chnéffléne to the frying pan with the sauce. Repeat this process until all the batter is cooked.

Gently stir the cooked chnéffléne to coat in the luscious sauce. Top with the reserved crispy guanciale, grated parmigiano and parsley, if using, and serve immediately.

CHNÉFFLÉNE

Chnéffléne (pronounced 'ke-nef-le-ne') is a traditional 12th—13th century dish from the Valle d'Aosta, originating from the German Walser community within the Gressoney Valley. It is also known as 'gnocchetti della Valle d'Aosta'. Chnéffléne resembles a teardrop-shaped dumpling made from a thick batter rather than pasta dough, which is pushed through a perforated tool directly into boiling water. The batter is similar to German or Austrian spätzle, using only eggs, milk and flour, although a lighter version can be made using water instead of milk.

Pasta alla Valdostana

✳
Serves
6
✳

This cheesy, creamy pasta dish reflects the strong dairy heritage of the alpine Aosta Valley. I've used packaged penne to save time and keep the focus on the Fontina cheese, which defines the dish. Pasta alla Valdostana can include mushrooms and a hint of nutmeg, which are both delicious additions, but this version of the dish is a simpler, more traditional version.

- 50 g (1¾ oz) unsalted butter
- 300 g (10½ oz) prosciutto cotto or ham, diced or roughly chopped
- 200 ml (7 fl oz) cream (35% fat), plus extra as needed
- 250 g (9 oz) Fontina, diced or chopped
- 500 g (1 lb 2 oz) dried penne
- grated Parmigiano Reggiano, to serve (optional)

Bring a large saucepan of water to the boil over high heat.

Meanwhile, start on the sauce. In a large frying pan over medium heat, cook the butter until just melted, then add the prosciutto cotto and saute, stirring occasionally, for around 5 minutes, until browned on all sides.

Add the cream and Fontina to the frying pan mixture. Stir until melted and fully combined. Reduce the heat to low and season with salt and pepper to taste.

Once the saucepan of water is boiling, add cooking salt and the penne and cook for 2 minutes less than the packet instructions.

Use a handled colander to transfer the pasta directly into the cheesy cream sauce. Stir to combine and coat the pasta completely. Add some extra cream if required – you want the sauce to be quite loose at this stage. Finish cooking the pasta and sauce together over medium heat for 2 minutes, to allow the sauce to reduce slightly and the flavours to mesh perfectly.

Serve immediately, topped with grated parmigiano if you wish.

Note

If the sauce has split, simply add a ladle of pasta water and a dash of extra cream and stir vigorously to combine. This will help the cream to stabilise and re-emulsify into a creamy, cohesive sauce.

PASTA ALLA VALDOSTANA

The phrase 'alla valdostana' translates to 'in the style of the Aosta Valley'. The dish is usually made with penne, a Ligurian pasta shape, but the Valle d'Aosta has adopted the shape in this rich and creamy dish. Of course, you can use different pasta shapes if you wish; rigatoni, fettuccine or fusilloni would all make a suitable choice.

Fontina is the traditional cheese used in pasta alla valdostana. This cow's milk cheese has a mild, nutty flavour and melts easily (and brings the ultimate comfort food feel). Fontina is classified as a DOP product, which means only milk from the Aosta Valley can be used to make cheese labelled as 'Fontina DOP'. If you're unable to source Fontina, you can substitute it with provolone dolce, gouda or Taleggio cheeses.

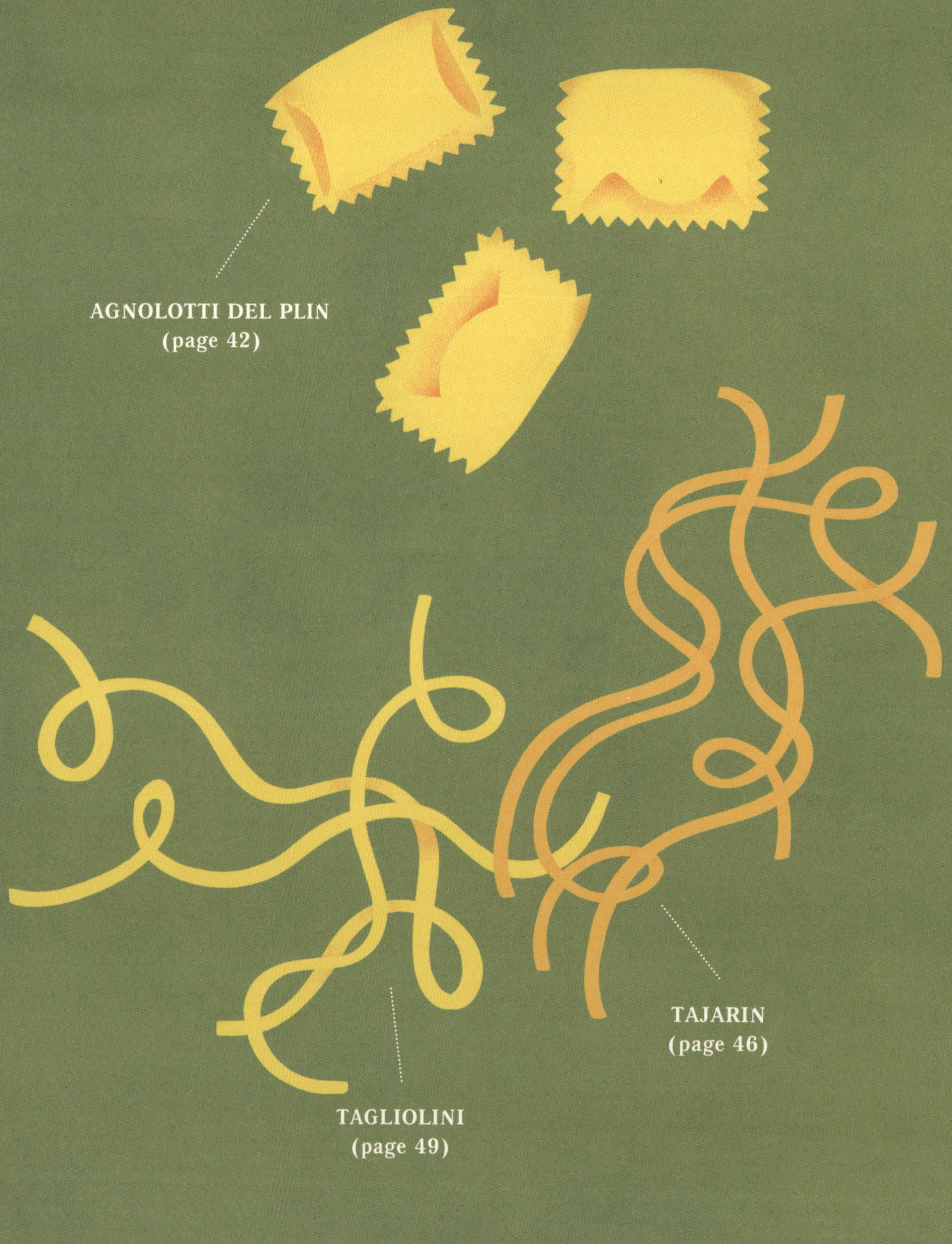
AGNOLOTTI DEL PLIN
(page 42)
TAJARIN
(page 46)
TAGLIOLINI
(page 49)

PIEMONTE

Piemonte, or Piedmont, is the second-largest Italian region, spanning from the Alps to the Mediterranean. It's known for its elegant cities, including the capital, Turin. Turin is a city with a regal history – it is home to the Palazzo Reale (Royal Palace of Turin), the main residence of the House of Savoy in the 16th century. This influential royal family played a major role in Italy's unification. The palace still holds historical and cultural significance and in 1946 it was converted to a museum and became a UNESCO World Heritage Site in 1997.

The Piemonte region boasts rich, fertile soil where trees bearing chestnuts and hazelnuts flourish. The soil is also used to grow nutritious feed for grazing cattle, which produce high-quality milk. Castelmagno, gorgonzola and robiola cheeses all hail from Piemonte, and are staples in dishes of the region. The regional cattle breed, razza Piemontese, is known for its tender meat. You'll often see fassona beef on the menu here, sometimes prepared in a dish called vitello tonnato – a typical Piemonte dish of cold sliced veal in a creamy tuna or anchovy and caper sauce.

Locals draw from these rich ingredients to create hearty dishes, often combining both meat and cheese together, and typically using butter instead of olive oil for cooking. The dishes pair well with the region's renowned wine varieties, with Barolo being an especially celebrated style from the region.

Piemonte is also the heart of the Slow Food movement, which promotes the principles and protection of regional food traditions with a focus on local and seasonal ingredients. This movement supports small businesses and farmers with initiatives active throughout Italy.

Pasta dishes from this region embrace the use of butter, nuts, wine and spices such as nutmeg in their sauces, and some are filled with leftover roasted meat, which was an important process in the 'no waste' attitude of Italian kitchens. As for pasta shapes – tagliolini or tagliarini (or 'tajarin', as it is known in dialect), maccheroni and agnolotti del plin are all from this region.

Agnolotti del plin con burro e salvia

AGNOLOTTI WITH BUTTER AND SAGE

✶
Serves
4
✶

For my take on this classic Piemonte recipe, I use beef combined with spinach and spices in a traditional style. Agnolotti del plin can be made with either leftover roasted meat or minced meat of your choice. I have outlined both methods here.

Pasta tools

pasta machine or rolling pin
pasta cutter

Filling

25 g (1 oz) unsalted butter
100 ml (3½ fl oz) dry white wine
1 small onion, finely chopped
1–2 garlic cloves, crushed
1 rosemary sprig, leaves only, finely chopped
100 g (3½ oz) spinach or cabbage, finely chopped
½ teaspoon freshly grated or ground nutmeg
500 g (1 lb 2 oz) roasted beef, diced, or minced (ground) beef (see Note)
1 egg (about 55 g/2 oz), lightly beaten
50 g (1¾ oz) Parmigiano Reggiano, grated, plus extra to serve

Pasta

400 g (14 oz) 00 flour, plus extra for dusting
4 eggs (about 220 g/8 oz total)
pinch of salt

Sauce

100 g (3½ oz) unsalted butter
handful of sage leaves, washed and dried

For the filling

If using roasted beef, first melt the butter in a frying pan over medium heat, then add the wine, onion, garlic, rosemary, spinach and nutmeg. Cook for 5 minutes, then add the diced beef and season with salt and pepper to taste. Remove from heat and allow to cool slightly.

If using minced beef, heat a large frying pan over medium heat, add the mince to the dry pan and cook for about 7–8 minutes, until browned. Add the butter, wine, onion, garlic and rosemary and cook for 5–6 minutes, until the onion has softened. Add the spinach and nutmeg and cook until the leaves have wilted. Season with salt and pepper to taste. Remove from the heat and set aside to cool slightly.

With either mixture, once cooled, transfer to a food processor or finely chop by hand to form a rough paste. Add the beaten egg and parmigiano, mix well and set aside.

For the pasta

Mix, knead and rest the pasta ingredients following the instructions on pages 17–18. Place the rested dough on a work surface that has been lightly dusted with 00 flour and divide into four portions. Cover the portions so they don't dry out.

Working with one portion at a time, roll the dough into sheets using a pasta machine (see pages 18–21) or by hand (pages 21–22). Roll the pasta sheets to a thickness of 1.5 mm (1/16 in). Depending on your pasta machine, this may be setting 6 or 7.

Place the pasta sheet on a lightly floured surface with the long edge facing you. Cut the pasta sheet in half lengthwise.

Place one teaspoon of the filling about 3–4 cm (1¼–1½ in) in from the long edge of the pasta sheet. Repeat, leaving about 3–4 cm (1¼–1½ in) between each teaspoon of filling. When you have mounds of filling along the whole length of the pasta sheet, fold the pasta sheet over the filling to meet the opposite long edge, enclosing the filling. ➥

Pinch the top layer of pasta firmly between each mound of filling to seal, making sure to press between and around each mound to remove any air pockets. Use a pasta cutter to trim the excess pasta along the long edge where the two layers of pasta sheet meet. You want approx. 1 cm (½ in) of pasta between the filling and the cut edge of the pasta sheet.

With the folded edge facing you, use the pasta cutter to cut between the agnolotti to separate them. Cutting away from you (from the folded edge towards the cut edge) will cause the agnolotti to slightly fold over itself, which will create the signature look.

Place the agnolotti onto a tray that has been lightly dusted with flour. Repeat the rolling, filling and cutting process with the remaining dough portions and filling, then set aside until ready to cook.

To cook the agnolotti and make the sauce

Bring a large saucepan of water to the boil over high heat, then add cooking salt. Add the agnolotti and cook for 4–5 minutes, or until al dente.

Meanwhile, melt the butter in a large frying pan over medium heat. Add the sage leaves and cook for 2–3 minutes, until fragrant, then remove from the heat.

Use a handled colander to transfer the cooked pasta directly into the butter and sage sauce. Toss gently to coat, adding a little pasta water if needed for extra creaminess. Season to taste.

Serve immediately, topped with grated parmigiano.

Note

Feel free to adapt the meat to suit your preferences, you can use minced beef, veal or pork – or a combination of any of these!

AGNOLOTTI DEL PLIN

Legend has it that this pasta was created for a festa (party) after a Piemonte castello (castle) successfully defended itself during a siege. The chef — named Angeloto — had limited ingredients, so he roasted the meat he could find, used it to fill pasta, and made a sauce from the leftover meat bones.

'Plin' means 'pinch' in the Piedmontese dialect. The pasta sheet is folded lengthwise over small mounds of filling and pinched to create little square pockets before cutting in between each filled pocket to seal and separate them.

Agnolotti del plin may be served in brodo (broth), with a meaty sugo (sauce) or sugo d'arrosto (roasted meat jus), or pan-fried in butter and sage, sometimes finished with shaved truffle.

Tajarin con burro, salvia e limone

TAJARIN WITH BUTTER, SAGE AND LEMON

*
Serves
4
*

Tajarin is traditionally served with white truffle but I prefer the balance of butter, sage and lemon in this dish – no need to go truffle-hunting during the short seasonal window. The creamy butter sauce, with sage and a hint of citrus, make this a perfect dish to enjoy year-round.

Pasta tools

pasta machine with tajarin attachment (see Note) or rolling pin and pasta knife

Pasta

400 g (14 oz) 00 flour, plus extra for dusting
12 egg yolks
20 ml (¾ fl oz) extra virgin olive oil
pinch of salt
fine semolina flour, for dusting

Sauce

250 g (9 oz) unsalted butter
large handful of sage leaves
zest and juice of 1 lemon

To serve

crispy sage leaves
grated Parmigiano Reggiano

For the pasta

Mix, knead and rest the pasta ingredients (excluding the semolina flour) following the instructions on pages 17–18. Place the rested dough on a work surface that has been lightly dusted with 00 flour and divide into four portions. Cover the portions so they don't dry out.

Working with one portion at a time, roll the dough into sheets using a pasta machine (see pages 18–21) or by hand (pages 21–22). Roll the pasta sheets to a thickness of 1.5 mm (1⁄16 in). Depending on your pasta machine, this may be setting 6 or 7.

Let the pasta sheets rest on the work surface for a few minutes to slightly dry before cutting. Lightly dust a tray with fine semolina flour or have your pasta drying rack nearby.

If using a pasta machine to cut the tajarin, fit the tajarin attachment to your pasta machine. Pass the pasta sheet through the attachment, gently picking up the cut strands and laying them onto the tray or rack. Repeat this process for the remaining dough portions, then set aside until ready to cook.

If cutting the tajarin by hand, lay the pasta sheet on the work surface with the short edge facing you. Lightly dust the pasta sheet with fine semolina flour and fold the pasta sheet loosely a few times along the entire length of the sheet, so you have a folded tube of dough with many layers. Gently flatten the tube, then cut the dough into strips 2 mm (approx. 1⁄16 in) wide with a knife. Unroll the strips and lay them onto the tray or rack. Repeat this process for the remaining dough portions, then set aside until ready to cook. ➥

For the sauce
Heat the butter in a large frying pan over medium heat until it bubbles. Add the sage leaves and cook, stirring occasionally, for 2–3 minutes, until crispy. Reduce heat to low, remove the sage and set aside on kitchen paper.

Add the lemon juice to the frying pan and heat through. Season to taste with salt and pepper.

To cook the tajarin and serve
Bring a large saucepan of water to the boil over high heat, then add cooking salt. Add the tajarin and cook for 4–5 minutes, until al dente.

Use a handled colander to transfer the cooked tajarin directly into the sauce. Gently mix to coat, adding a little pasta water if needed for extra creaminess.

Top with lemon zest, crispy sage and grated parmigiano.

Note
The tajarin pasta machine attachment can be sourced online or from homeware or kitchen supply stores that specialise in pasta tools.

TAJARIN

Tajarin (pronounced 'tah-yah-REEN') is the regional dialect name for tagliarini, from the word 'tagliare', meaning 'to cut'. Tajarin is traditionally made with a rich dough of egg yolks — often around three yolks to every 100 g (31/2 oz) flour — and may be either hand- or machine-rolled. This long, thin and delicate pasta is usually rolled into a very fine pasta sheet and then cut into narrow strips about 2 mm (approx. 1/16 in) wide.

While usually matched with white truffle when in season, it is also perfect with mushrooms, with simple sauces such as burro, salvia e limone (butter, sage and lemon), or with fresh tomato sauce.

Tagliolini con gamberoni e zucchine

TAGLIOLINI WITH KING PRAWNS AND ZUCCHINI

✳
Serves
4
✳

There are so many sauces that can be matched with tagliolini, so I have decided to combine seafood with vegetables for this recipe. If king prawns are not available, then mussels or vongole (clams) can be used. As we are cooking with seafood, cheese isn't included in the recipe; instead, the dish is finished with some fresh parsley and a bit of chilli.

Pasta tools

pasta machine with tagliolini attachment (see Notes) or rolling pin and pasta knife

Pasta (see Notes)

400 g (14 oz) 00 flour (see Notes), plus extra for dusting
4 eggs (about 220 g/8 oz total)
pinch of salt
fine semolina flour, for dusting

Sauce

100 ml (3½ fl oz) extra virgin olive oil, plus extra as needed
12–16 raw king prawns (jumbo shrimp), deveined and peeled, heads and shells reserved
2 small zucchinis (courgettes), halved lengthwise then thinly sliced into half moons
3 garlic cloves, roughly chopped
125 ml (½ cup) dry white wine, preferably from Piemonte (see Notes)

To serve

handful of parsley leaves, chopped
chilli flakes (optional)

For the pasta

Mix, knead and rest the pasta ingredients (excluding the semolina flour) following the instructions on pages 17–18. Place the rested dough on a work surface that has been lightly dusted with 00 flour and divide into four portions. Cover the portions so they don't dry out.

Working with one portion at a time, roll the dough into sheets using a pasta machine (see pages 18–21) or by hand (pages 21–22). Roll the pasta sheets to a thickness of 2 mm (approx. $\frac{1}{16}$ in). Depending on your pasta machine, this may be setting 5 or 6.

Let the pasta sheet rest on the work surface for a few minutes to slightly dry before cutting. Lightly dust a tray with fine semolina flour or have your pasta drying rack nearby.

If using a pasta machine to cut the tagliolini, fit the tagliolini attachment to your pasta machine. Pass the pasta sheet through the attachment, gently picking up the cut strands and laying them onto the tray or rack. Repeat this rolling and cutting process for the remaining dough portions, then set aside until ready to cook.

If cutting the tagliolini by hand, lay the pasta sheet on the work surface with the short edge facing you. Lightly dust the pasta sheet with fine semolina flour and fold the pasta sheet loosely a few times along the entire length of the sheet, so you have a folded tube of dough with many layers. Gently flatten the tube, then cut the dough into strips 2 mm (approx. $\frac{1}{16}$ in) wide with a knife. Unroll the strips and lay them onto the tray or rack. Repeat this rolling and cutting process for the remaining dough portions, then set aside until ready to cook.

For the sauce

In a large frying pan over medium heat, add the olive oil and the prawn heads and shells. Saute for a few minutes until all the flavours have infused. Remove the heads and shells from the pan and discard.

Add a little more oil to the pan if needed, then add the prawns and saute for 3–4 minutes, until cooked through. Remove the prawns from the pan and set aside.

In the same frying pan, add the zucchini and garlic and saute for 3 minutes, until the zucchini starts to soften. Add the white wine and cook for another 3 minutes, then reduce the heat while you cook the pasta.

To cook the tagliolini and finish the sauce
Bring a large saucepan of water to the boil over high heat, then add cooking salt. Add the tagliolini and cook for 3 minutes, or until al dente.

One minute before the pasta is cooked, return the cooked prawns to the frying pan with the sauce.

Use tongs to lift and transfer the cooked tagliolini directly into the sauce and gently mix to combine. Season to taste with salt and pepper.

Serve immediately, topped with the chopped parsley and some chilli flakes if you wish.

Notes
The tagliolini pasta machine attachment can be sourced online or from homeware or kitchen supply stores that specialise in pasta tools.

There are different flour options you can try when making fresh tagliolini; you can use just 00 flour, as I have in this recipe, or a 50:50 combination of fine semolina flour and 00 flour, which will give a firmer, more rustic texture.

You can use dried tagliolini pasta instead of fresh if you wish. You'll need about 500 g (1 lb 2 oz) for this recipe. Simply cook the dried pasta according to the packet instructions.

If you can source wine from Piemonte, I recommend using a dry white wine such as timorasso or Roero Arneis.

TAGLIOLINI

Tagliolini is shared by several regions, including Piemonte in the north and Molise in the south. Using the same base dough as many fresh egg pastas, it is a delicate, long and finely cut ribbon shape. It is generally paired with simple sauces such as limone (lemon) and olive oil or chilli and olive oil, or seasonal verdure (vegetables) — but it can also be served with seafood or tartufo (truffles).

Tagliolini con gamberoni e zucchine ✶ *Tagliolini with king prawns and zucchini*

CORZETTI
(page 56)
TROFIE
(page 63)
TRENETTE
(page 60)
PENNE
(page 64)
FAZZOLETTI
(page 66)

LIGURIA

Liguria is the third-smallest Italian region, with its narrow terrain stretching between the Alps and the Apennines, and characterised by beautiful beaches and dramatic cliffs. Its capital, Genoa, is known as the port city, while Portofino, Sanremo and Cinque Terre are the cities that can be found along a stretch of coastline known as the Italian Riviera.

Cinque Terre draws visitors to Liguria every year, and is populated by picturesque villages and colourful houses that were painted by fishermen so they could see their homes while at sea. The name Cinque Terre translates to 'five villages', which are Monterosso, Vernazza, Corniglia, Manarola and Riomaggiore. Each village has its own spectacular coastal views, beaches and restaurants.

Genoa played an important role in maritime trade over the centuries, and you'll see a fair bit of seafood in its dishes. It's also the birthplace of pesto alla Genovese, which dates as far back as the 16th century, and is used in many iconic pasta dishes. The city also boasts a rich variety of pasta shapes, such as pansotti, which translates to 'pot-belly', a triangular pasta shape that is filled with wild greens and served in a walnut sauce.

Over many years, the Liguria region has experienced a rise and fall in economic status, which means that when cattle became scarce, locals sourced alternatives such as fish, chestnuts, chickpeas (garbanzo beans), pine nuts, walnuts and herbs for their meals.

Liguria has some unique pasta shapes that sometimes require specific pasta-making tools. For instance, corzetti is a pasta that resembles a coin and uses a hand-carved wooden stamp to be formed; while the long, slightly rounded strands of trenette were originally rolled by hand but today are commonly made using a specifically designed pasta roller attachment. Other Ligurian shapes require nothing more than your hands (and maybe a pasta cutter) to make them. Trofie is still hand-rolled today (but it's one of the harder shapes for me to master!); and a favourite of mine, fazzoletti di seta (silk handkerchief pasta), looks much harder to make than it is!

Corzetti

CORZETTI

Corzetti takes its name from a 14th-century Genoese coin, called a corzetto. This pasta is traditionally made using carved wooden stamps that emboss a design on a thin, coin-shaped disc. During the Italian Renaissance, noble families embraced corzetti as a way to display their wealth and status — the stamps featured family crests, names or coats of arms. The stamps were traditionally hand-made by local artisans and passed down through families.

Corzetti con olio, pinoli e maggiorana

CORZETTI WITH OLIVE OIL, PINE NUTS AND MARJORAM

*
Serves
6
*

Corzetti dough is made with white wine, which gives the pasta a silky texture. It can be served with many sauces, but traditionally it was simply paired with olive oil, as I've recreated here. Once you start making corzetti, you'll catch yourself pausing to admire how beautiful the shape is … I always do!

Pasta tools

pasta machine or rolling pin
corzetti stamps (see Note)

Pasta

400 g (14 oz) 00 flour, plus extra for dusting
3 eggs (about 165 g/6 oz total) or 5 egg yolks
50 ml (1¾ fl oz) dry white wine
pinch of salt
fine semolina flour, for dusting

Sauce

125 ml (½ cup) extra virgin olive oil, or as needed
100 g (3½ oz) pine nuts or walnuts, toasted
small bunch of marjoram or oregano

To serve

grated Parmigiano Reggiano (optional)

For the pasta

Mix, knead and rest the pasta ingredients (excluding the semolina flour) following the instructions on pages 17–18. Place the rested dough on a work surface that has been lightly dusted with 00 flour and divide into four portions. Cover the portions so they don't dry out.

Working with one portion at a time, roll the dough into sheets using a pasta machine (see pages 18–21) or by hand (pages 21–22). Roll the pasta sheet to a thickness of 2–3 mm (1/16–1/8 in). Depending on your pasta machine, this may be between setting 3 or 6.

Dust the corzetti stamp with fine semolina flour. Using the flat cutter side of the stamp, cut out discs from the pasta sheet. Press each disc firmly between the two patterned halves of the stamp to emboss the design. Remove carefully and place the corzetti onto a tray that has been lightly dusted with fine semolina flour. Repeat the rolling and shaping process with the remaining dough portions, then set aside until ready to cook.

To cook the corzetti and make the sauce

Bring a large saucepan of water to the boil over high heat, then add cooking salt. Add the corzetti and cook for about 5 minutes – they're ready when they float to the surface, but taste one to check.

While the corzetti are cooking, heat the olive oil in a frying pan over medium heat. Add the toasted nuts and marjoram and saute for 1–2 minutes, until fragrant.

Use a slotted spoon or handled colander to lift and transfer the cooked corzetti directly into the sauce. Stir gently to coat the corzetti in the sauce. To serve, top with the pine nuts and grated parmigiano, if using.

Note

Corzetti stamps can be sourced online or from homeware or kitchen supply stores that specialise in pasta tools.

Trenette al pesto alla Genovese

TRENETTE WITH BASIL PESTO

✶
Serves
4
✶

A traditional basil pesto is my favourite way to serve trenette – I particularly love it topped with a touch of chilli. I've provided two methods for making the pesto alla Genovese: the traditional way, using a mortar and pestle, or with a food processor. If you have the time, I really recommend trying the traditional way – it produces an amazing flavour that does not compare to pesto made in a food processor!

Pasta tools

pasta machine with trenette attachment (see Notes)

Pasta (see Notes)

400 g (14 oz) 00 flour (see Notes), plus extra for dusting
4 eggs (about 220 g/ 8 oz total)
pinch of salt
fine semolina flour, for dusting

Pesto alla Genovese

2–3 garlic cloves, peeled
pinch of salt
2 bunches of basil, leaves picked
50 g (1¾ oz) pine nuts, toasted
50 g (1¾ oz) Grana Padano or Parmigiano Reggiano, finely grated, plus extra to taste
125 ml (½ cup) extra virgin olive oil

To serve

grated Parmigiano Reggiano
chilli flakes (optional)

For the pasta

Mix, knead and rest the pasta ingredients (excluding the semolina flour) following the instructions on pages 17–18. Place the rested dough on a work surface that has been lightly dusted with 00 flour and divide into four portions. Cover the portions so they don't dry out.

Working with one portion at a time, roll the dough into sheets using a pasta machine (see pages 18–21). Roll the pasta sheet to a thickness of 2 mm (0.08 in). Depending on your pasta machine, this may be setting 5 or 6.

Let the pasta sheets rest on the work surface for a few minutes to slightly dry before cutting. Lightly dust a tray with fine semolina flour or have your pasta drying rack nearby.

Fit the trenette attachment to your pasta machine. Pass the pasta sheet through the attachment, gently picking up the cut strands and laying them onto the tray or rack. Repeat this process for the remaining pasta sheets, then set aside until ready to cook.

For the pesto

If using a mortar and pestle to make the pesto, place the garlic and salt into the mortar and pound until the garlic is crushed and fully broken down. Add the basil leaves in three additions, pounding the mixture gently until a thick paste forms. After the final basil addition, add the pine nuts, half of the cheese and a little olive oil and mix with the pestle for around 3–5 minutes, until incorporated. The timing of this process will depend on how coarse or fine you want your pesto to be.

If using a food processor to make the pesto, place the garlic in the bowl of your food processor and pulse a few times until finely minced. Add the basil leaves and gently pulse until the leaves are finely chopped or the mixture forms a thick paste. ➥

Make sure you do not overprocess at this stage as it will darken the pesto. Add the pine nuts, half of the cheese and a little olive oil and pulse until fully incorporated. At this stage, taste your pesto then add salt and more cheese as needed. Continue to drizzle in olive oil and either stir or pulse until fully emulsified and to your desired texture. Transfer to a bowl or jar and top with olive oil to prevent the surface drying out.

See Notes (below) for information on storing leftover pesto in the fridge or freezer.

To cook the trenette and finish the sauce

Bring a large saucepan of water to the boil over high heat, then add cooking salt. Add the trenette and cook for 3–4 minutes, or until al dente.

In a large bowl, add 60–80 ml (¼–⅓ cup) of basil pesto.

Use a handled colander to transfer the cooked trenette directly into the pesto and gently mix to combine. Any pasta water carried over with the trenette will gently warm the pesto and add a little creaminess too.

Serve immediately, topped with grated parmigiano. I also like to add some chilli flakes on top, but this is optional.

Notes

The trenette attachment can be sourced online or from homeware or kitchen supply stores that specialise in pasta tools.

There are different flour options for fresh trenette; you can use just 00 flour, as I have in this recipe, or a 50:50 combination of fine semolina flour and 00 flour, which will give a firmer, more rustic texture.

As dried trenette can be difficult to source outside of Italy, you can substitute dried linguine or tagliatelle for the fresh trenette if you prefer. You'll need about 500 g (1 lb 2 oz) for this recipe. Cook the dried pasta according to the packet instructions.

Homemade pesto can be stored in an airtight jar or container in the fridge for up to 5 days. Make sure to cover the top of the pesto with a thin layer of olive oil – this provides a protective layer that prevents the pesto from oxidising and discolouring.

To freeze pesto, portion into small containers or an ice cube tray and freeze. Thaw in the fridge overnight or melt gently in a pan over low–medium heat.

TRENETTE

Trenette is a long, thin pasta with a slightly oval profile, originating from Genoa. A staple in the region since at least the 13th century, it was originally rolled by hand but is now made using a special pasta machine attachment.

Trenette is typically served with pesto alla Genovese – either on its own or with green beans and potatoes (see page 62).

Trofie con fagiolini, patate e pesto

TROFIE WITH GREEN BEANS, POTATO AND PESTO

✳
Serves
6
✳

This recipe is another traditional Ligurian way of serving pesto alla Genovese. The beautiful trofie spirals are cooked together with green beans and potatoes, with a generous amount of pesto added just before serving.

Pasta
400 g (14 oz) fine semolina flour, plus extra for dusting
200 ml (7 fl oz) lukewarm water
pinch of salt

Sauce
3 all-purpose potatoes (about 500 g/1 lb 2 oz total), peeled and cut into 1.5–2 cm (½–¾ in) cubes
200 g (7 oz) green beans, trimmed and cut into 2.5 cm (1 in) lengths
80 ml (⅓ cup) Pesto alla Genovese (page 59), or as needed

To serve
grated Grana Padano or Parmigiano Reggiano (optional)

For the pasta
Mix, knead and rest the pasta ingredients following the instructions on pages 17–18. Place the rested dough on a work surface and divide into six portions. Cover the portions so they don't dry out. If the dough is very sticky, knead the dough for a few minutes longer and rest for a further 10 minutes before you move on to shaping the trofie.

Working with one portion at a time, pinch a piece of dough about the size of a sultana or a hazelnut. Place the dough under the palm of your hand and, using medium pressure, roll the dough away from you, so it becomes a skinny rope with slightly tapered ends.

Readjust your hand over the dough so that the outer edge of your palm is touching one of the tapered edges. In one continuous movement, drag your palm and the dough diagonally towards you. This action should cause the side of your palm to create a spiral twist in the pasta dough. It takes a bit of practice to master this shape so don't be discouraged if you don't get it straight away!

Place the trofie onto a tray that has been lightly dusted with fine semolina flour. Repeat the rolling and shaping process with the remaining dough portions, then set aside until ready to cook.

To cook the vegetables and trofie and serve
Bring a large saucepan of water to the boil over high heat, then add cooking salt. Add the potatoes and cook for 3 minutes, or until the potatoes just start to soften.

Add the trofie and cook for another 3 minutes. Add the beans and cook a final 2 minutes, until the pasta is al dente.

Reserve 250 ml (1 cup) of the cooking water, then drain the pasta and vegetables. Return the pasta and vegetables to the pan off the heat. Add the pesto and gently stir to coat. Add a little of the reserved cooking water, gently stirring again to loosen the sauce as needed. Taste and adjust seasoning.

Serve topped with grated Grana Padano, if desired.

TROFIE

Trofie originated in Golfo Paradiso, a stretch of coastline on the Italian Riviera, particularly in the small villages of Sori, Recco, Uscio and Camogli. Women in these villages would create these twisted jewels for their families and to sell them on to nearby restaurants. The pasta didn't become widely common until the 1960s, when it started to be marketed across Italy.

The name 'trofie' comes from the Italian 'strufuggia' and the Ligurian Genoese 'strofissia', meaning 'to rub'. The small, short, twisted pasta with pointed ends is hand-rolled using a dough made from fine semolina flour and water. In winter, some villages would mix 00 flour and chestnut flour when wheat was in short supply.

Penne al pomodoro

PENNE IN TOMATO SAUCE

Serves 6

Penne is traditionally served with pesto, creamy sauces or a simple pomodoro (tomato) sauce. I love tomatoes so I've included my take on penne al pomodoro, using dried penne, given it's so abundant and easy to source.

- 80–125 ml (⅓–½ cup) extra virgin olive oil
- 4 garlic cloves, finely chopped or crushed
- 800 g (1 lb 12 oz) tinned cherry or whole peeled tomatoes
- small bunch of basil
- 500 g (1 lb 2 oz) dried penne pasta
- 150 g (5½ oz) Parmigiano Reggiano or Pecorino Romano, grated, plus extra to serve

For the sauce

Heat the olive oil in a large frying pan over medium heat. Add the garlic and cook until softened but not browned.

Add the tomatoes, then roughly tear the basil leaves and add them to the pan. You can also include the basil stalks if you wish – they will add extra flavour as they cook.

Bring the sauce to the boil, stirring well, then reduce the heat to low and simmer for about 15 minutes while you cook the penne, stirring occasionally. Taste and season with salt and pepper. You can remove the basil stalks before finishing if you wish, but it's also fine to leave them in.

To cook the penne and serve

Bring a large saucepan of water to the boil over high heat, then add cooking salt. Add the penne and cook according to the packet instructions.

Use a handled colander to transfer the cooked pasta directly into the sauce and toss to coat, adding a little pasta water if needed for extra creaminess. Add half the grated parmigiano and stir through. Top with the remaining cheese and serve, with even more cheese on the side if you desire.

PENNE

Penne is one of the most versatile pasta shapes, found in kitchens around the world. The name translates to 'quill', 'feather' or 'pen', reflecting its angled, pointed, pen-like form. There are two main varieties: penne rigate (with ridges) and penne lisce (smooth). The pasta typically measures 3–5 cm (1¼–2 in) in length.

The shape dates back to 1865, when Giovanni Battista Capurro, a pasta maker from San Martino d'Albaro in Genoa, patented a machine that could extrude tubular pasta and cut it diagonally into short, even lengths. Penne was originally rolled and cut by hand using durum wheat and water, but thanks to Capurro's invention, production became faster and more consistent.

FAZZOLETTI

'Fazzoletti' means 'handkerchief', which feels fitting when you see the appearance of the silky, delicate pasta sheets for the first time. After being cut into large squares or rectangles and cooked, this shape gloriously folds and drapes on the plate.

One of the oldest and simplest pasta shapes, fazzoletti originated in the Ligurian capital of Genoa. In the local dialect this shape is called 'mandilli de saea' or 'fazzoletti di seta', meaning 'silk handkerchief'. Fazzoletti is usually served with pesto alla Genovese. You may find this on some restaurant menus but it's not a common dish — if you do, order it, you won't be disappointed.

Fazzoletti laminati con prezzemolo in olio, aglio e peperoncino

FAZZOLETTI LAMINATED WITH PARSLEY IN OLIVE OIL, GARLIC AND CHILLI

✳
Serves
6
✳

I'm sharing my favourite way to make fazzoletti – with a touch of pasta art! Laminating parsley leaves into the sfoglia (pasta sheet) is an easy way to make this simple pasta shape a showstopper. You can also use edible flowers or other soft herbs. I've opted to keep the sauce simple so we don't hide all that beautiful work.

Pasta tools

- pasta machine
- rolling pin
- pasta cutter (fluted or smooth)

Pasta

- 600 g (4 cups) 00 flour, plus extra for dusting
- 6 eggs (about 330 g/11½ oz total)
- pinch of salt
- bunch of parsley, leaves only, for laminating
- fine semolina flour, for dusting

Sauce

- 160 ml (⅔ cup) extra virgin olive oil
- 3–4 garlic cloves, chopped or crushed
- 2 red chillies, chopped, or 2 teaspoons chilli flakes, plus extra to serve

For the pasta

Mix, knead and rest the pasta ingredients (excluding the semolina flour) following the instructions on pages 17–18. Place the rested dough on a work surface that has been lightly dusted with 00 flour and divide into four portions. Cover the portions so they don't dry out.

Working with one portion at a time, roll the dough into sheets using a pasta machine (see pages 18–21). Roll the pasta sheet to a thickness of 1.5 mm (1⁄16 in). Depending on your machine, this may be setting 6 or 7.

Lay one sheet on a surface that has been lightly floured with 00 flour. Arrange the parsley leaves over the sheet, then place a second sheet on top. Gently press the two sheets together using a rolling pin. Pass the layered sheet back through the pasta machine on a slightly thicker setting – this may be setting 5 or 6.

Using a pasta cutter, cut the laminated pasta sheet into large squares or rectangle. Each side should be between. 7.5–10 cm (2¾–4 in). Place the fazzoletti onto a tray that has been lightly dusted with fine semolina flour. Repeat the rolling, laminating and cutting process with the remaining dough portions then set aside until ready to cook.

To cook the fazzoletti and serve

Bring a large saucepan of water to the boil over high heat, then add cooking salt. Add the pasta and cook for 4–5 minutes, or until al dente.

Meanwhile, heat the olive oil in a large frying pan over medium heat. Add the garlic and chilli and saute for 2–3 minutes, until fragrant, taking care not to brown the garlic.

Use a handled colander to carefully transfer the cooked fazzoletti into the frying pan and gently jiggle to coat in the oil sauce.

Serve immediately topped with extra chilli.

PIZZOCCHERI
(page 73)
SCARPINOCC
(page 76)
CASONCELLI
(page 79)
TORTELLI
(page 84)

LOMBARDIA

Lombardia's (or Lombardy's) name and history were influenced by the Lombards, a Germanic tribe who arrived in Italy in the 6th century, and played a significant role in the medieval development of Italy. The region, and its capital Milan, is now the leading industrial and commercial hub of Northern Italy. Although true of the whole region, Milan has become synonymous with high-end designers thanks to its prestigious fashion events and boutiques. Italian fashion houses such as Armani, Dolce & Gabbana, Gucci, Prada, Versace, Bottega Veneta and Valentino, just to name a few, have had global influence with their contributions, proving Italy's reputation as a leading centre for fashion.

The region is known for its cultural attractions (and Romanesque architecture), including the Duomo di Milano, the renowned Teatro alla Scala (Opera House), the Galleria Vittorio Emanuele II shopping arcade, Arco della Pace, the Sforzesco Castle and Santa Maria delle Grazie, where you can see Leonardo da Vinci's *The Last Supper*.

Lombardia also boasts a significant violin-making history; Cremona was the home of famous families — Amati, Stradivari and Guarneri. This craft is quite important to the region, and is recognised by UNESCO as an important part of its cultural heritage.

Pasta making is also an art form in Lombardia, and there are many unique shapes that are specific to the region, such as pizzoccheri, scarpinocc, casoncelli and tortelli. The pasta here is generally served with simple ingredients and uses butter as the base in many sauces. Just don't wear your designer clothes while you eat them.

Pizzoccheri della Valtellina

✳
Serves
4
✳

As the name suggests, this dish originates from the Valtellina valley. It's typically served with potatoes and cabbage, though silverbeet (Swiss chard) or green beans may be substituted depending on what's in season.

Buckwheat flour is gluten free and can be brittle if used on its own, so I've combined it with 00 flour for an easier to work with dough.

Pasta tools

pasta machine or rolling pin

1 small savoy cabbage (about 300 g/10½ oz), trimmed and cored
400 g (14 oz) all-purpose or baby (chat) potatoes, peeled and diced into 1.5 cm (½ in) chunks

Pasta

350 g (12½ oz) buckwheat flour
125 g (4½ oz) 00 flour, plus extra for dusting
250 ml (1 cup) water, plus extra as needed
pinch of salt
fine semolina flour, for dusting

Sauce

200 g (7 oz) unsalted butter
2–3 garlic cloves, roughly chopped
handful of sage leaves
200 g (7 oz) Valtellina Casera (or Fontina, or gouda), finely diced

To serve

grated Grana Padano or Parmigiano Reggiano (optional)

For the pasta

Mix, knead and rest the pasta ingredients (excluding the semolina flour) following the instructions on pages 17–18. Place the rested dough on a work surface that has been lightly dusted with 00 flour and divide into four portions. Cover the portions so they don't dry out.

Working with one portion at a time, roll the dough into sheets using a pasta machine (see pages 18–21) or by hand (pages 21–22). Roll the pasta sheet to a thickness of 2–3 mm (1/16–1/8 in). Depending on your pasta machine, this may be between setting 3 and 6.

Cut the pasta sheet into strips 1 cm (½ in) wide, then cut across the sheet to form ribbons about 8 cm (3¼ in) long. Place the pizzoccheri onto a tray that has been lightly dusted with semolina flour. Repeat the rolling and cutting process with the remaining dough portions, then set aside until ready to cook.

To cook the vegetables, pizzoccheri and make the sauce

Separate the leaves of the cabbage, slice them in half and then into strips about 2–3 cm (¾–1¼ in) wide.

Bring a large saucepan of water to the boil over high heat, then add cooking salt. Add the cabbage and potatoes and cook for 4–5 minutes.

Add the pizzoccheri to the same pot and cook for a further 3 minutes, until the pasta is al dente and the vegetables are tender.

While the pizzoccheri and vegetables are cooking, melt the butter in a large frying pan over medium heat. Add the garlic and cook until softened. Add the sage and cook for a further 2 minutes.

When the pasta and vegetables are cooked, reserve 250 ml (1 cup) of cooking water. Gently drain the pizzoccheri and vegetables, then add to the pan along with the reserved cooking water. Season to taste, then add the Valtellina Casera and gently stir through until the cheese has melted and combined with the sauce.

Serve immediately, topped with grated parmigiano if you wish.

PIZZOCCHERI

Pizzoccheri (pronounced 'pi-tso-ke-ri') is a semi-short, flat, chewy ribbon-shaped pasta commonly served as a hearty meal in the high mountain villages in Lombardia.

Buckwheat has been grown and harvested in the Valtellina since the 17th century, it is a northern Italian staple which is also found in cakes, breads and polenta nera (a variation of polenta, made from buckwheat instead of the traditional cornmeal).

The original recipe has been officially recognised and protected by the Academy of the Pizzoccheri in Teglio, which promotes awareness of this local tradition as a hallmark of Italian excellence.

Scarpinocc di Parre

*
Serves
6
*

I love the taste and texture of the rich fresh pasta used in this recipe. Traditionally, villagers used a rich filling made from local staples such as Grana Padano, breadcrumbs, butter, milk, eggs, garlic, herbs and spices, served simply in a butter and sage sauce.

Pasta tools

- pasta machine or rolling pin
- 8–9 cm (3¼–3½ in) round cutter (optional)

Filling

- 300 g (10½ oz) Grana Padano or Parmigiano Reggiano, grated, plus extra to serve
- 100 g (3½ oz) dried breadcrumbs
- pinch of salt
- ½ teaspoon ground nutmeg
- ½ teaspoon ground cinnamon
- 1 egg (about 55 g/2 oz)
- 30 g (1 oz) unsalted butter, melted
- 100 ml (3½ fl oz) full-cream (whole) milk

Pasta

- 300 g (2 cups) 00 flour, plus extra for dusting
- 80 g (2¾ oz) fine semolina flour, plus extra for dusting
- 2 eggs (about 110 g/4 oz total)
- 125 ml (½ cup) full-cream (whole) milk, plus extra as needed
- 25 g (1 oz) unsalted butter, melted
- pinch of salt

Sauce

- 150 g (5½ oz) unsalted butter
- small handful of sage leaves

For the filling

In a bowl, combine the cheese, breadcrumbs, salt, nutmeg and cinnamon. Add the egg and mix while slowly adding the melted butter.

Gradually add the milk and mix until the filling forms a semi-solid texture that can be rolled into walnut-sized balls. Set aside.

For the pasta

Mix, knead and rest the pasta ingredients following the instructions on pages 17–18. Place the rested dough on a work surface that has been lightly dusted with 00 flour and divide into four portions. Cover the portions so they don't dry out.

Working with one portion at a time, roll the dough into sheets using a pasta machine (see pages 18–21) or by hand (pages 21–22). Roll the pasta sheet to a thickness of 2–3 mm (1/16–1/8 in). Depending on your pasta machine, this may be between setting 3 or 6.

To roll and shape the scarpinocc

Cut the pasta sheet into small squares about 8 × 8 cm (3¼ × 3¼ in) in size or use a round cutter to cut discs 8–9 cm (3¼–3½ in) in diameter. Shape the scarpinocc using one of the following methods.

If using square-shaped pasta, place one of the small pasta squares in front of you. Spoon a heaped teaspoon of the filling in the centre of the edge that is closest to you. Fold the pasta over the filling in thirds so that the seam is on the bottom. With your index and thumb finger, pinch the ends firmly to seal, forming a ridge at the top that resembles wings. Press down gently in the centre to form an indent.

If using disc-shaped pasta, place one of the small pasta discs in front of you. Spoon a heaped teaspoon of the filling in the centre of the disc. Fold over into a half-moon, sealing tightly. Fold the sealed edge so that it sits under the filling. With your index and thumb fingers, pinch the sides firmly to seal, forming a ridge at the top that resembles wings. Press down gently in the centre to form an indent. ➥

Place the scarpinocc onto a tray that has been lightly dusted with fine semolina flour. Repeat the rolling, cutting and filling process with the remaining dough portions and filling, then set aside until ready to cook.

To cook the scarpinocc and make the sauce

Bring a large saucepan of water to the boil over high heat, then add cooking salt. Add the scarpinocc and cook for 5–6 minutes, or until al dente.

Meanwhile, in a large frying pan, melt the butter over medium heat. Add the sage leaves and cook for 2–3 minutes, until crispy. Reduce the heat to low.

Use a handled colander to transfer the cooked scarpinocc directly into the butter sauce. Gently toss to coat, season to taste with salt and pepper and add a little pasta water if needed, to add a little extra creaminess.

Top with grated Grana Padano to serve.

SCARPINOCC

Scarpinocc (pronounced 'skar-pee-nohtch') originated in the village of Parre, in the province of Bergamo on the slopes of the Trevasco and Alino mountains. The name comes from 'scarpa' – meaning 'shoe' – because the unusual filled pasta shape resembles the handcrafted cloth shoes once worn by local shepherds and villagers up until the mid-20th century.

The dough is quite rich, made from 00 and fine semolina flours, milk, eggs, salt and melted butter. Traditionally it was hand-rolled into long ropes, cut into gnocchi-sized pieces and rolled into discs approximately 6–8 cm (2½–3¼ in) in diameter. However, I have also found recipes that roll the dough to a 2–3 mm (1/16–1/8 in) thickness to create a large sheet, then cut round discs or squares to fill and create the scarpinocc shape.

This filled pasta holds deep local significance – it is traditionally made on 29 June to celebrate the feast of the village patron Saint Peter. There's even an annual Scarpinocc festival held in August where locals queue for delicious specialty plates to devour.

CASONCELLI

Also called 'casonsèi' in the local dialect, casoncelli dates back to the 14th century. The pasta dough is rolled very thin to showcase the filling, which historically made use of leftovers to avoid waste. Fillings varied according to the status of the family: poorer families would use was available – their fillings might include seasonal vegetables, cheaper cuts of meat or offal and breadcrumbs. More affluent families might use meat, ricotta, cheeses such as Grana Padano or Parmigiano Reggiano, sultanas, raisins, pear, spinach, pumpkin, masala or even amaretti biscuits.

Shapes differ between villages – from half-moon to a shape similar to scarpinocc (page 75) – but my favourite (and the closest to the traditional form) looks like a folded handkerchief or little aeroplane wings.

There isn't one 'official' recipe for casoncelli. Instead, each village (and often each family) has its own version, for example:

- Casoncelli alla Bergamasca (from the Province of Bergamo)
  The filling usually includes roast veal, pork, breadcrumbs, eggs, Parmigiano Reggiano, garlic and parsley. The pasta is typically served with burro e salvia (butter and sage) and topped with pancetta and extra cheese.

- Casoncelli di Barbariga (from the Province of Barbariga)
  This is a true expression of the territory. Fillings vary but may include breadcrumbs, Parmigiano Reggiano and Grana Padano, butter, prosciutto cotto, meat or vegetable stock, spinach, nutmeg, sage, parsley, sultanas, pear or butter.
  This pasta shape is a protected local product under the Municipal Designation of Origin, recognised by the Municipality of Barbariga through the approval of specific production regulations.

- Casoncelli della Valle Camonica (from the Province of Brescia)
  Fillings vary but can include meat or vegetables. In the town of Longhena, locals usually make the filling with spinach or silverbeet (Swiss chard).

Casoncelli alla Bresciana

*
Serves
4
*

My favourite version of this dish is from the Province of Brescia. The filling is made with stale breadcrumbs and Grana Padano and the pasta is served simply in burro e salvia (butter and sage), topped with extra cheese.

The dough can be made with either water or olive oil – both result in a thin, delicate texture, although I prefer the olive oil version.

Pasta tools

pasta machine or rolling pin

Filling

100 g (3½ oz) unsalted butter
2 garlic cloves, crushed
1 tablespoon chopped parsley
½ teaspoon grated or ground nutmeg
150 g (5½ oz) coarse breadcrumbs (see page 236)
2–3 amaretti biscuits, crushed
100 g (3½ oz) Grana Padano, grated
80–100 ml (2½–3½ fl oz) Brodo (page 116), as required

Pasta

400 g (14 oz) 00 flour, plus extra for dusting
4 eggs (about 220 g/8 oz total)
20 ml (¾ fl oz) water or extra virgin olive oil
pinch of salt
fine semolina flour, for dusting

Sauce

80 g (2¾ oz) unsalted butter
handful of sage leaves
2–3 amaretti biscuits, crushed (optional)
80 g (2¾ oz) Grana Padano, grated

For the filling

In a frying pan over medium heat, melt the butter, then add the garlic and saute for 1–2 minutes. Add the parsley, nutmeg, breadcrumbs, amaretti and Grana Padano. Season with salt to taste.

Gradually add just enough broth to create a soft but thick mixture, stirring to incorporate. Set aside to cool.

For the pasta

Mix, knead and rest the pasta ingredients (excluding the semolina flour) following the instructions on pages 17–18. Place the rested dough on a work surface that has been lightly dusted with 00 flour and divide into four portions. Cover the portions so they don't dry out.

Working with one portion at a time, roll the dough into sheets using a pasta machine (see pages 18–21) or by hand (pages 21–22). Roll the pasta sheet to a thickness of 2 mm (approx. 1/16 in). Depending on your pasta machine, this may be setting 5 or 6.

To roll and shape the casoncelli

Cut the pasta sheets into 8 × 8 cm (3¼ × 3¼ in) squares.

Place 1 teaspoon of filling in the centre of each square. Fold one corner over to almost meet the opposite edge (but not all the way), sealing lightly – use a dab of water if needed.

Lift up the edge containing the filling and roll it over towards the centre. You should see three pointed edges: one small point above the filling and a pointed 'wing' on each side. Press each wing down to seal, taking care not to press the filled centre, so it appears full and puffed.

Place the casoncelli onto a tray that has been lightly dusted with fine semolina flour. Repeat the rolling, cutting and filling process with the remaining dough portions and filling, then set aside until ready to cook. ➥

To cook the casoncelli and make the sauce

Bring a large saucepan of water to the boil over high heat, then add cooking salt. Cook the casoncelli for 5–6 minutes, or until al dente.

Meanwhile, in a large frying pan, melt the butter over medium heat. Add the sage leaves and cook for 2–3 minutes, until crispy. Reduce the heat to low.

Use a handled colander to transfer the cooked casoncelli directly into the butter sauce. Gently toss to coat, season to taste with salt and pepper and add a little pasta water if needed, to add a little extra creaminess.

Take the mixture off the heat and stir through the crushed amaretti biscuits, if using.

Top with grated Grana Padano or parmigiano and serve immediately.

Tortelli con zucca

✳
Serves
4
✳

Tortelli con zucca is also known as 'tortelli mantovani'. The filling typically includes roasted pumpkin, mostarda, amaretti and nutmeg – flavours that match perfectly together. Mostarda is a northern Italian condiment of whole candied fruits in a mustard syrup. It provides a sweet-and-spicy element, but can be substituted with marmalade if you cannot source it.

Pasta tools

pasta machine or rolling pin
fluted pasta cutter or square pasta stamp (optional)

Filling

500 g (1 lb 2 oz) butternut pumpkin (squash), peeled, deseeded and diced
5–6 amaretti biscuits, crushed
40 g (1½ oz) mostarda (optional)
50 g (1¾ oz) Grana Padano, grated
½ teaspoon grated nutmeg
½ teaspoon salt, or to taste
½ teaspoon freshly ground black pepper, or to taste

Pasta

400 g (14 oz) 00 flour, plus extra for dusting
4 eggs (about 220 g/8 oz total)
pinch of salt
fine semolina flour, for dusting

Sauce

100 g (3½ oz) unsalted butter
handful of sage leaves

To serve

grated Grana Padano or Parmigiano Reggiano
amaretti biscuits, crushed (optional)

For the filling

Preheat the oven to 180°C (350°F). Arrange the pumpkin on a large baking tray and bake for 30–40 minutes, or until soft and cooked through. Remove from the oven and mash or puree with a fork or food processor. Set aside to cool.

In a bowl, combine the pumpkin mash, amaretti, mostarda, if using, Grana Padano, nutmeg, salt and pepper. Mix well and set aside.

For the pasta

Meanwhile, mix, knead and rest the pasta ingredients (excluding the semolina flour) following the instructions on pages 17–18. Place the rested dough on a work surface that has been lightly dusted with 00 flour and divide into four portions. Cover the portions so they don't dry out.

Working with one portion at a time, roll the dough into sheets using a pasta machine (see pages 18–21) or by hand (pages 21–22). Roll the pasta sheet to a thickness of 1.5 mm (1/16 in). Depending on your pasta machine, this may be setting 6 or 7.

To roll and shape the tortelli

Shape the tortelli using one of the following methods.

For the fold-over method, place 1 teaspoon of filling about 1–2 cm (½–¾ in) in from the long edge of the pasta. Repeat along the pasta sheet leaving a gap of 3 cm (1¼ in) between each teaspoon of filling. Fold the pasta sheet over the filling to meet the other edge, then press between each mound and around the filling to remove any air pockets. Cut the tortelli using a fluted pasta cutter or square stamp.

For the pre-cut squares method, cut the pasta sheet into even 7 × 7 cm (2¾ × 2¾ in) squares. Place a teaspoon of filling in the centre of each, place the second square on top and seal the edges – a light brush of water can help with sealing. Make sure to press between each mound and around the filling to remove any air pockets. ➥

Place the tortelli onto a tray that has been lightly dusted with fine semolina flour. Repeat the rolling, cutting and filling process with the remaining dough portions and filling, then set aside until ready to cook.

To cook the tortelli and make the sauce
Bring a large saucepan of water to the boil over high heat, then add cooking salt. Add the tortelli and cook for 4–5 minutes, or until al dente.

Meanwhile, melt the butter in a large frying pan over medium heat. Add the sage leaves and cook for 2–3 minutes, until crispy. Reduce the heat to low. Remove the sage, place on paper towel and set aside.

Use a handled colander to transfer the cooked tortelli directly into the sauce. Gently toss to coat, adding a little pasta water if needed for extra creaminess. Season to taste with salt and pepper.

Serve immediately, topped with crispy sage, grated Grana Padano and crushed amaretti, if desired.

TORTELLI

'Tortelli' is a word that is used to describe a number of filled pasta shapes across Italy, but it originates from Mantua, near the three lakes of Lago Superiore, Lago di Mezzo and Lago Inferiore. In this region, it is traditionally filled with zucca (pumpkin/squash) and nutmeg.

Many Italians argue about which shape is the correct version of tortelli – round, square, half-moon or twisted like tortelloni (a larger version of tortellini). Some people even use the term interchangeably with ravioli!

Tortelli is considered a gastronomic specialty and holds an important place in this historically Catholic country, often being served at Christmas Eve dinner in the regions of Lombardia, Emilia-Romagna, Toscana and Umbria.

SCHLUTZKRAPFEN
(MEZZELUNE)
(page 91)

SPÄTZLE TIROLESI
(page 93)

TRENTINO-ALTO ADIGE / SÜDTIROL

Before World War I, the Trentino-Alto Adige/Südtirol region was part of the Austro-Hungarian Empire, also called the Dual Monarchy (1867–1918), a state composed of two sovereign entities under a single ruling monarch. Following the collapse of the empire at the end of World War I, Trentino-Alto Adige was annexed by Italy. As a result, the region's culture reflects both German linguistic influence and a strong Austrian heritage, particularly in Alto Adige (also known as Südtirol), where many people still speak and write in German and local dialects retain Germanic roots. In contrast, Trentino, to the south, has a more distinctly Italian Alpine culture.

The capital, Trento, is home to notable architecture, including Trento Cathedral with its Gothic-Romanesque design, and historic buildings featuring Renaissance and Venetian elements, such as Palazzo Thun. The city also embraces contemporary architecture, most notably the Museo delle Scienze (also called the MUSE), which was designed by Renzo Piano, while nearby alpine towns such as Canazei in Val di Fassa are renowned ski destinations.

These combined cultural influences are also reflected in the region's food. Dishes tend to be rich and hearty, often featuring polenta and cured meats such as speck, with clear Austrian and Central European influences alongside Italian traditions. Pasta dishes, too, reflect this crossover, with names such as spätzle tirolesi, canederli (bread dumplings), schlutzkrapfen (mezzelune) and casunziei.

Schlutzkrapfen di ricotta, patate e spinaci in burro marrone ✶ *Ricotta, potato and spinach schlutzkrapfen in brown butter*

Schlutzkrapfen di ricotta, patate e spinaci in burro marrone

RICOTTA, POTATO AND SPINACH SCHLUTZKRAPFEN IN BROWN BUTTER

✳
Serves
6
✳

When researching this region of Italy, I was intrigued by both the name of this pasta and the use of buckwheat or rye flours, which lend a nutty flavour and rustic texture to the pasta dough. I tend to alternate between the two flours when making this pasta at home.

Pasta tools

pasta machine or rolling pin
8–9 cm (3¼–3½ in) round cutter

Filling

80 ml (⅓ cup) extra virgin olive oil
400 g (14 oz) spinach
pinch of salt
80 g (2¾ oz) all-purpose potatoes, peeled
80 g (2¾ oz) ricotta, drained
1 garlic clove, crushed
1 small onion, finely chopped
30 g (1 oz) Parmigiano Reggiano, grated
½ teaspoon grated or ground nutmeg

Pasta

250 g (9 oz) 00 flour, plus extra for dusting
150 g (5½ oz) buckwheat or rye flour
4 eggs (about 220 g/8 oz total)
20 ml (¾ fl oz) extra virgin olive oil
pinch of salt
fine semolina flour, for dusting

For the filling

Heat the olive oil in a frying pan over medium heat, then add the spinach and salt, and saute until the leaves have wilted. Remove from the pan and leave to cool slightly. Squeeze out any excess liquid, then finely chop the spinach and set aside to cool.

Meanwhile, boil the potato in salted water and cook for 15 minutes, or until fully cooked. Drain and mash the potato and set aside to cool.

In a large bowl, combine the spinach, mashed potato, ricotta, garlic, onion, parmigiano and nutmeg. Mix until fully combined and season with salt and pepper. Set aside.

For the pasta

Mix, knead and rest the pasta ingredients (excluding the semolina flour) following the instructions on pages 17–18. Place the rested dough on a work surface that has been lightly dusted with 00 flour and divide into four portions. Cover the portions so they don't dry out.

Working with one portion at a time, roll the dough into sheets using a pasta machine (see pages 18–21) or by hand (pages 21–22). Roll the pasta sheet to a thickness of 1.5 mm (1/16 in). Depending on your pasta machine, this may be setting 6 or 7.

To roll and shape the schlutzkrapfen

Place a pasta sheet on your lightly floured work surface. Cut discs using a round cutter about 8–9 cm (3¼–3½ in) in diameter.

Place 1 teaspoon of filling in the centre of each disc. Fold over to form a half-moon and press to seal, crimping the edges with a fork.

Sauce
150 g (5½ oz) unsalted butter, plus extra to serve

To serve
grated Parmigiano Reggiano

Place the schlutzkrapfen onto a tray that has been lightly dusted with fine semolina flour. Repeat the rolling, cutting and filling process with the remaining dough portions and filling, then set aside until ready to cook.

To cook the schlutzkrapfen and make the sauce
Bring a large saucepan of water to the boil over high heat, then add cooking salt. Add the schlutzkrapfen and cook for 4–5 minutes, or until al dente.

Meanwhile, melt the butter in a large frying pan over medium heat Reduce the heat to low.

Use a handled colander to transfer the cooked pasta directly into the butter sauce. Gently toss to coat, adding a little pasta water only if needed for silkiness. Season to taste with salt before serving.

Serve immediately topped with a little extra melted butter and grated parmigiano.

PASTA TOUR · ITALY · ITALY ·

SCHLUTZKRAPFEN (MEZZELUNE)

A half-moon filled pasta similar to ravioli or pierogi, schlutzkrapfen originated in the Tyrol and South Tyrol regions, and is also found in Austria. The German name (pronounced 'shloots-krahp-fen') and Italian name (mezzelune) are both commonly used in recipes and restaurants.

The dough often combines flours such as 00 flour, buckwheat or rye with fine semolina flour, eggs and olive oil. In the South Tyrol area, it's common to use a combination of 00 and rye flours, which makes the dough easier to knead. The filling is usually ricotta, potato and spinach, though variations often include cheese, mushrooms or meat. This pasta is typically served with pesto, sausages or in a luscious browned butter sauce.

Spätzle tirolesi in salsa cremosa con Asiago e speck croccante

DUMPLINGS IN A CREAM SAUCE WITH ASIAGO AND CRISPY SPECK

*
Serves
4
*

This spätzle tirolesi is another comfort dish that I could devour a second serving of very easily! Here I have topped it with speck or pancetta, but you can finish the spätzle with chopped walnuts for a vegetarian variation.

Pasta tools

spätzle-style perforated tool or sturdy metal colander

Pasta

150 g (1 cup) 00 flour, plus extra as needed
½ teaspoon freshly grated or ground nutmeg
2 eggs (about 110 g/4 oz total)
30 ml (1 fl oz) full-cream (whole) milk, plus extra as needed
250 g (9 oz) cooked spinach (about 500 g/1 lb 2 oz fresh), drained, finely chopped and cooled (see page 90)
pinch of salt

Sauce

50 g (1¾ oz) unsalted butter
1 onion, finely chopped
80 g (2¾ oz) speck or pancetta, thinly sliced into batons
100 ml (3½ oz) cream (35% fat), plus extra as needed

To serve

grated Asiago or Stelvio (see Note)

For the pasta

In a large bowl, whisk together half the flour with the rest of the pasta ingredients until fully combined.

Gradually add the remaining flour as needed, while whisking continuously, until a thick but pliable batter forms. Set aside to rest for 20–30 minutes. Loosen with a little extra milk if it becomes too thick or add a little more flour if it becomes too thin – we are aiming for a thick, pancake-batter-style consistency.

For the sauce

While the batter rests, heat the butter in a large frying pan over medium heat. Add the onion and cook until softened. Add the speck and saute until browned. Remove from the heat until ready to finish.

To cook the spätzle

Bring a large saucepan of water to the boil, then add cooking salt. Working over the boiling water, pour a ladleful of batter into the spätzle-style tool and push/slide it through the holes so the batter drops directly into the water. This will create the 'teardrop' shape.

Cook for 2–3 minutes, until the spätzle rise to the surface. Use a handled colander to transfer the cooked spätzle to the frying pan with the sauce. Gently stir through the sauce to coat.

Repeat until all the batter is used.

To finish and serve

Return the frying pan to low heat, pour in the cream and heat through. Add extra cream or a little pasta water if needed to loosen the sauce. Taste and adjust seasoning.

Serve immediately, topped with grated Asiago or Stelvio.

Note

The two regional cheeses used in this dish – Asiago and Stelvio – are both DOP products. If they are unavailable, Parmigiano Reggiano is a good alternative.

SPÄTZLE TIROLESI

Spätzle tirolesi, also known as 'spinatspatzeln' (pronounced 'shpeh-tza-tel-n'), is the Italian version of the German spätzle. The dough consistency is closer to a thick batter than a traditional pasta dough, so there is some debate as to whether it's actually pasta or a dumpling.

As with chnéffléne (page 34), the batter, which has been enriched with spinach and nutmeg, is pushed through a perforated tool directly into boiling water, forming small teardrop-shaped pieces.

CJARSONS
(page 97)
BLECS
(page 103)

FRIULI-VENEZIA GIULIA

The region of Friuli-Venezia Giulia has been fought over by many: the Romans in 181 BCE; the Slavs, who migrated after the fall of the Roman Empire in 476 CE; the Venetians, who gained control of Friuli in the 15th century; and the Austrians, who dominated much of the region after the Treaty of Campo Formio in 1797, when Venice surrendered to the Habsburg Monarchy. The region's name reflects this jumbled make-up — 'Friuli' comes from the Latin term Forum Iulium (meaning 'Julius [Caesar]'s marketplace'). Caesar founded a forum in this region in the mid-1st century BCE, in a town which is today known as Cividale del Friuli. 'Venezia Giulia' was suggested as part of the region's name in an attempt to mark the Italian cultural spirit of the area. It also reflects the Julian Alps, which border the east of the region.

In 1954, following World War II, the current borders of the region were decided, and Trieste was incorporated into Italy as part of Friuli-Venezia Giulia. This tangled history has created an amalgamation of languages, cultures and cuisines. The range of climates from alpine to Mediterranean allows for a colourful food where hearty, comfort mountain dishes meet Mediterranean meals. The region has two large rivers, the Tagliamento and the Isonzo, which are both major sources of freshwater fish, which show up in many dishes typical of Friuli-Venezia Giulia. The region's historic and neighbouring influences, including the Roman, German and Slavic cultures, have all contributed to the choice of ingredients and unique cooking styles.

CJARSONS

Cjarsons (pronounced 'KYAR-sons') is a rich filled pasta from Friuli in the Carnia and Timau areas of Udine. It was originally created as a festive dish that dates back to around the 14th or 15th century. One of the earliest recorded recipes appears in the 15th-century cookbook *Libro de Arte Coquinaria* by Maestro Martino da Como, a renowned culinary figure. In his text, the pasta was originally called 'calisciconi', though you'll see many name variations — including cjalsons, cialzons and cialcions — depending on the village and dialect.

The dough is made with potatoes, similar to gnocchi, but shaped like agnolotti, half-moon ravioli or even rolled into small filled balls. Some variations use a flour-and-water dough, either with or without eggs, but the potato-based dough is considered the original version.

Cjarsons is known for its distinctive mix of flavours — savoury, sweet or both. Each village, and often each family, has its own signature filling, handed down through generations (and kept secret from outsiders). There is no single 'correct' recipe — each variation reflects local ingredients, history and family tradition. Examples include:

- Cjarsons di Paularo (from the town of Paularo)
  Filled with fresh ricotta, cherry jam, cocoa and rum.
- Cjarsons di Treppo Carnico (from the village of Treppo Carnico)
  Typically filled with mashed red potatoes, onion, bacon and shallots.

The dish is celebrated with Giornata Nazionale dei Cjarsons (National Cjarsons Day), a national day recognising its cultural importance and its many regional interpretations.

Cjarsons ripieni di spinaci e ricotta, con burro e ricotta affumicata

CJARSONS FILLED WITH SPINACH AND RICOTTA IN BUTTER AND SMOKED RICOTTA

✳
Serves
6
✳

Gnocchi is one of my favourite Italian dishes, and potato is one of my favourite ingredients, so this filled half-moon pasta with a potato dough stood out to me when I was researching this book. These beautiful sweet and savoury dumplings, served simply in butter with a dusting of cinnamon on top, are pure perfection.

Pasta tools

potato ricer
rolling pin
6–7 cm (2½–2¾ in) round cutter

Pasta

1 kg (2 lb 3 oz) starchy potatoes (such as russet, Sebago, King Edward or desiree)
1 egg (about 55 g/2 oz), lightly beaten
pinch of salt
250 g (9 oz) 00 flour, or as needed
fine semolina flour, for dusting

Filling

100 g (3½ oz) cooked spinach (about 200 g/7 oz fresh), drained, finely chopped and cooled (see page 90)
300 g (10½ oz) ricotta, drained
½ apple, grated
½ teaspoon ground cinnamon
pinch of salt

Sauce

200 g (7 oz) unsalted butter
40 ml (1¼ fl oz) extra virgin olive oil

For the pasta

Place the potatoes in a saucepan of cold water, cover and bring to the boil over medium-high heat. Reduce to medium heat and simmer for 25–30 minutes, or until cooked through. Drain and set aside to cool for 10 minutes, then peel.

Pass the potatoes through a ricer onto a clean work surface or into a large bowl. Add the egg, salt and 150 g (1 cup) of the flour. Mix gently with your hands, adding more flour as needed until a very soft but cohesive dough forms. The exact amount of flour you will need will depend on your potatoes; you will know you have the right consistency when the dough becomes smooth and can be easily rolled and shaped.

Knead lightly on a floured surface until smooth and pliable, dusting with more a little more flour if the dough is sticky.

To make the filling and shape the cjarsons

In a bowl, combine the spinach, ricotta, apple, cinnamon and salt. Mix well and set aside.

Lightly dust a work surface with fine semolina flour and use a rolling pin to roll the potato dough into one large sheet until about 5 mm (¼ in) thick. Cut discs using a round cutter 6–7 cm (2½–2¾ in) in diameter.

Place a teaspoon of filling in the centre of each disc, fold over to form a half-moon and press the curved edge with a fork to seal.

Place the cjarsons onto a tray that has been lightly dusted with fine semolina flour. Repeat the filling process with the remaining dough and filling, then set aside until ready to cook.

To serve
ground cinnamon (optional)
crumbled smoked ricotta (optional; see Note)

For the sauce
Heat the butter and olive oil in a large frying pan over medium heat for about 6–8 minutes, until the butter is foaming gently. Reduce the heat to low, being careful not to burn the butter.

To cook the cjarsons and serve
Meanwhile, bring a large saucepan of water to the boil over high heat, then add cooking salt. Add the cjarsons and cook for 4–5 minutes, or until they rise to the surface.

Use a handled colander to transfer the cooked cjarsons directly into the sauce. Toss gently to coat, adding some pasta water into the sauce if needed for extra creaminess.

Serve immediately, drizzled with the butter sauce and topped with a dusting of cinnamon or crumbled smoked ricotta, if using.

Note
Ricotta affumicata (smoked ricotta) can usually be found at well-stocked Italian delis. If it's not readily available, an alternative would be a crumbled semi-soft cheese such as smoked caciotta.

Cjarsons ripieni di spinaci e ricotta, con burro e ricotta affumicata ✶
Cjarsons filled with spinach and ricotta in butter and smoked ricotta

Blecs in burro e Montasio

BLECS IN BUTTER AND MONTASIO

✳
Serves
4
✳

Blecs have traditionally been served with butter and the local cheese Montasio, sometimes topped with a few crispy sage leaves. I've included this simple and delicious recipe to highlight the nutty flavour of the buckwheat pasta.

Pasta tools

pasta machine or rolling pin

Pasta

350 g (12½ oz) 00 flour, plus extra for dusting
150 g (5½ oz) buckwheat flour
4 eggs (about 220 g/8 oz total)
50 g (1¾ oz) unsalted butter, softened
pinch of salt
fine semolina flour, for dusting

Sauce

150 g (5½ oz) unsalted butter
12–14 sage leaves

To serve

grated Montasio or Parmigiano Reggiano

For the pasta

Mix, knead and rest the pasta ingredients (excluding the semolina flour) following the instructions on pages 17–18. Place the rested dough on a work surface that has been lightly dusted with 00 flour and divide into four portions. Cover the portions so they don't dry out.

Working with one portion at a time, roll the dough into sheets using a pasta machine (see pages 18–21) or by hand (pages 21–22). Roll the pasta sheet to a thickness of 2 mm (approx. 1/16 in). Depending on your pasta machine, this may be setting 5 or 6.

Cut the pasta sheet into off-cut, irregular shapes and place the blecs onto a tray that has been lightly dusted with fine semolina flour. Repeat the rolling and cutting process with the remaining dough portions, then set aside until ready to cook.

To cook the blecs and make the sauce

Bring a large saucepan of water to the boil over high heat, then add cooking salt. Add the blecs and cook for 3–4 minutes, or until al dente.

Meanwhile, melt the butter in a large frying pan over medium heat until it bubbles. Add the sage leaves and cook until crispy. Remove a few sage leaves and set aside on a plate lined with paper towel until ready to serve.

Use a large handled colander to transfer the cooked blecs directly into the butter sauce. Toss gently to coat, adding a little pasta water if needed for extra creaminess. Season to taste with salt and pepper.

Serve immediately, drizzled with extra butter sauce and topped with the reserved crispy sage leaves and the grated Montasio cheese.

BLECS

Also called 'biechi' or 'bleki', 'blecs' is the local dialect name for this pasta and translates loosely to 'odd cut' or 'patchwork pieces'. The pasta originated near the Slovenian and Austrian borders and is made from a rustic dough that combines 00 and buckwheat flours, although today you find some simpler versions are made using only 00 flour.

The buckwheat flour gives this pasta a nutty, earthy taste, while the addition of 00 flour allows this pasta shape to remain delicate. Blecs is often served with a bold red wine sauce made from local Friulian red wine called 'tazzelenghe' which has been cooked down with guanciale and butter over nearly 2 hours. Here, I've decided to highlight a quicker, but equally delicious, butter and sage sauce.

CASUNZIEI
(page 111)
BIGOLI
(page 108)

VENETO

Veneto's capital, Venice, is renowned for its canals and gondolas, the islands of Murano and Burano, Piazza San Marco, cicchetti (small snacks) and world-class wines. Stretching from the Dolomites to the Adriatic Sea, the region is also home to other well-loved cities, including Verona, Padua, Vicenza and Treviso. Veneto also borders Italy's largest lake, Lake Garda, which it shares with the regions of Lombardia in the north-west and Trentino-Alto Adige in the north.

The region's cuisine is varied; however, pasta is not traditionally the main dish here (though bigoli and pappardelle are commonly found on Venetian tables). Instead, the region is known for its abundance of seafood, rice, polenta and vegetables — particularly radicchio and Castelfranco lettuce, as well as mushrooms and artichokes. Beef, duck and even horse meat are also served as primary meats in regional dishes.

Veneto is home to several important products and ingredients classified as DOP, meaning they are produced within specific geographic areas using defined, approved techniques. These include some of my favourite Italian wines and cheeses, such as Prosecco, Asiago, Grana Padano, Piave and Casatella Trevigiana — all of which pair perfectly with pasta.

Bigoli in salsa

✳
Serves
4
✳

In this recipe, 'salsa' simply means 'sauce'. Bigoli is most commonly served in a salsa made from onions and anchovies or sardines, where the onions are slowly cooked down to form a creamy sauce. As there is no meat, this dish has traditionally been eaten on religious fasting days, such as Good Friday and Ash Wednesday.

Pasta tools

pasta machine with bigoli attachment or bigolaro tool (see Notes)

Pasta (see Notes)

300 g (2 cups) 00 flour, plus extra for dusting
200 g (7 oz) fine semolina flour, plus extra for dusting
4 duck eggs (about 232 g/8 oz total; see Notes)
20 ml (¾ fl oz) extra virgin olive oil or 20 g (¾ oz) unsalted butter, softened
50 ml (1¾ fl oz) full-cream (whole) milk or water
pinch of salt

Sauce

100 ml (3½ fl oz) extra virgin olive oil
1 large onion, halved and thinly sliced
50 ml (1¾ fl oz) dry white wine
10 anchovy fillets in oil

To serve

handful of parsley, chopped

For the pasta

Mix, knead and rest the pasta ingredients following the instructions on pages 17–18. Place the rested dough on a work surface that has been lightly dusted with 00 flour and divide into two portions. Cover the portions so they don't dry out.

If using a pasta machine to cut the bigoli, working with one portion at a time, roll the dough into sheets using a pasta machine (see pages 18–21). Roll the pasta sheet to a thickness of 2 mm (approx. 1⁄16 in). Depending on your machine, this may be setting 5 or 6.

Fit the bigoli attachment to your pasta machine. Pass the pasta sheet through the bigoli attachment, gently picking up the cut strands and laying them on to a tray that has been lightly dusted with fine semolina flour. Repeat rolling and cutting process for the remaining dough portion, then set aside until ready to cook.

If using a bigolaro to shape the bigoli, load one portion of the dough into the cylinder. Depending on the size of the cylinder you may need to cut the portion in half again. Turn the handle to push the dough through the die. Cut the bigoli to the desired length and place the strands onto a tray that has been lightly dusted with fine semolina flour. Repeat with the remaining dough portion, then set aside until ready to cook.

For the sauce

Heat the oil in a large frying pan over medium heat, then add the onion and saute until softened but not browned.

Add the wine and cook until it reduces slightly.

Add the anchovies and some of the anchovy oil and stir until the anchovies have completely dissolved into the sauce. Taste and season with salt and pepper, if needed. ➥

To cook the bigoli and serve

Meanwhile, bring a large saucepan of water to the boil over high heat, then add cooking salt. Cook the bigoli for 4–5 minutes, or until al dente.

Use a handled colander to transfer the bigoli directly into the sauce and gently mix to coat, adding a little pasta water if needed for creaminess. Sprinkle with a little chopped parsley to serve.

Notes

A bigolaro (or a bigoli attachment for your pasta machine) can be sourced online or from homeware or kitchen supply stores that specialise in pasta tools.

If you are not able to source duck eggs, you can use extra-large chicken eggs instead.

You can use dried pasta instead of fresh if you prefer. You'll need about 500 g (1 lb 2 oz) of bigoli or wholemeal (whole-wheat) spaghetti. Cook according to the packet instructions.

BIGOLI

Bigoli is a long, rough-textured, spaghetti-style pasta believed to have originated in Padua in the 14th century, although the exact date is debated. Traditionally, it was made from wholemeal (whole-wheat) or semolina flour that has been enriched with butter and duck eggs.

The history of the pasta's shape is slightly complicated. It was produced with a brass extruder called a 'bigolaro' (also known as a 'torchio'), which was invented and patented by Francesco Bottene in 1875. However, in 1604 Bartolomio Veronese was also credited for a version of the machine — a wooden, cylindrical press with a manual lever used to push the dough through. Bottene, though, is generally celebrated for preserving and standardising the pasta shape.

Casunziei all'Ampezzana

CASUNZIEI FILLED WITH BEETROOT

✶
Serves
4
✶

This beautiful pasta is filled with a beetroot mix and served in a simple butter sauce that is then topped with grated Parmigiano Reggiano and poppy seeds. The earthiness of the beetroots is the true highlight of this dish. I recommend roasting them, which creates a sweeter flavour.

Pasta tools

pasta machine or rolling pin
8 cm (3¼ in) round cutter

Filling

2 beetroots (beets) (about 500 g/1 lb 2 oz; see Note)
extra virgin olive oil, for drizzling
2 small starchy potatoes (about 200 g/7 oz), peeled
1 small parsnip (about 80 g/ 2¾ oz), peeled and ends trimmed
½ teaspoon freshly ground nutmeg
½ teaspoon salt

Pasta

300 g (2 cups) 00 flour, plus extra for dusting
3 eggs (about 165 g/6 oz total)
40 ml (1¼ fl oz) full-cream (whole) milk
pinch of salt
fine semolina flour, for dusting

Sauce

150 g (5½ oz) unsalted butter
50 g (1¾ oz) Parmigiano Reggiano, grated, plus extra to serve
1 tablespoon poppy seeds

For the filling

Preheat the oven to 200°C (400°F). Clean and trim the beetroot but leave the skins on. Cut into halves or quarters depending on size. Place them on an oven tray, coat with a little olive oil and roast for about 45–60 minutes, until tender. While still warm, puree the beetroot, with the skins still on, using a food processor or stick blender until smooth.

Alternatively, you can boil the beetroots. Add the cleaned, halved or quartered beetroots to a saucepan, cover with cold water and bring to a boil over high heat. Add 1 teaspoon salt, cook until tender, about 30–40 minutes, and drain. While still warm, puree until smooth.

While the beetroot is cooking, boil the potatoes and parsnips in a separate saucepan and cook until tender. Drain the potatoes and parsnips and remove from their skins while warm. Mash with a fork or potato ricer until smooth. Set aside the mashed potato and parsnip to cool completely.

In a bowl, combine the beetroot puree with the mashed potatoes and parsnips and mix well. Add the nutmeg and salt and season to taste.

For the pasta

Mix, knead and rest the pasta ingredients (excluding the semolina flour) following the instructions on pages 17–18. Place the rested dough on a work surface that has been lightly dusted with 00 flour and divide into four portions. Cover the portions so they don't dry out.

Working with one portion at a time, roll the dough into sheets using a pasta machine (see pages 18–21) or by hand (pages 21–22). Roll the pasta sheet to a thickness of 1.5 mm (1/16 in). Depending on your pasta machine, this may be setting 6 or 7.

To cut and shape the casunziei

Using a round cutter about 8 cm (3¼ in) in diameter, cut discs from the pasta sheets and place 1–1½ teaspoons of the filling in the centre of each disc. ➥

Fold each disc into a half-moon shape and seal the edges by pressing gently or crimping with a fork. If required, dab a little water around the edges to help seal before folding.

Place the casunziei onto a tray that has been lightly dusted with fine semolina flour. Repeat the rolling, cutting and filling process with the remaining dough portions and filling, then set aside until ready to cook.

To cook the casunziei and make the sauce

Bring a large saucepan of water to the boil over high heat, then add cooking salt. Cook the casunziei for 4–5 minutes, or until al dente.

Meanwhile, heat the butter in a large frying pan over medium heat until melted but not browned. Turn the heat off, add the parmigiano and half of the poppy seeds and stir through.

Use a handled colander to transfer the casunziei directly into the sauce. Gently stir to coat, adding a little pasta water if needed for creaminess.

To serve, drizzle over a little of the melted butter sauce, and sprinkle over the remaining poppy seeds and some extra grated parmigiano.

Note

It's always best to use fresh beetroots for maximum flavour as pre-cooked or tinned beetroot may alter the texture and flavour. If pre-cooked beetroot is the only available option, drain and remove as much of the liquid as possible and roast the beetroot briefly to reduce excess moisture.

CASUNZIEI

Casunziei is a vibrant filled pasta from the village of Cortina d'Ampezzo in the Dolomites. The name has Latin origins, though the pasta is known by many different spellings (including casonciei, casanzes and csanzöi) depending on the village or family.

Casunziei is half-moon shaped and typically filled with local seasonal vegetables, which might include beetroot, potatoes, spinach, mint, onion, turnips or chives. Traditionally, the pasta was served in winter, so the original filling was a combination of potato, beetroot and turnip; however, I prefer to substitute parsnip for turnip for some extra sweetness.

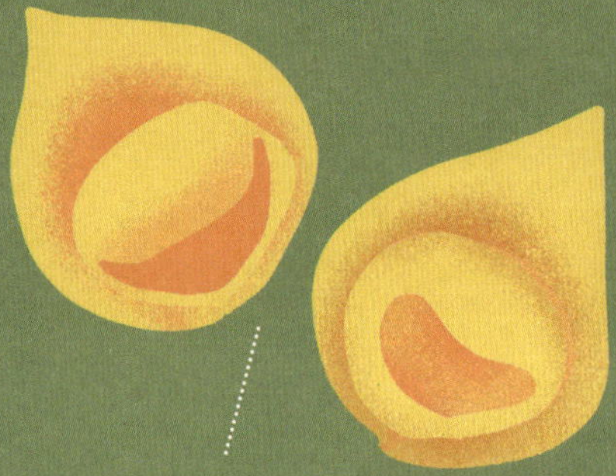

TORTELLINI
(page 114)

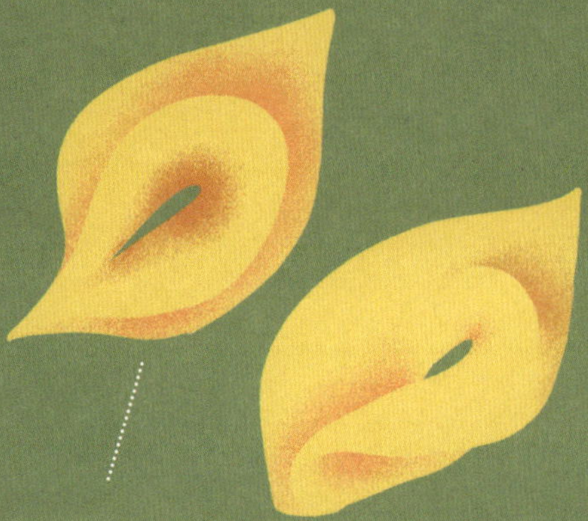

SORPRESINE
(page 120)

STROZZAPRETI
(page 122)

TAGLIATELLE
(page 126)

SPOJA LORDA
(page 130)

GARGANELLI
(page 135)

EMILIA-ROMAGNA

Emilia-Romagna extends from the Apennines to the Po River and is known for its medieval cities and seaside resorts. The capital, Bologna, dates back to the 11th century and is known by three nicknames: La Rossa (the Red), referring to its terracotta roofs and red-brick buildings; La Dotta (the Learned), as the home of the Università di Bologna, the oldest university in Europe; and La Grassa (the Fat), a reflection of the region's extraordinary food culture. It is a favourite destination for food lovers, celebrated for specialties such as traditional tortellini and mortadella.

This food-centric region is home to several key cities and iconic ingredients. Modena is renowned as the home of traditional balsamic vinegar, while Parma, as its name suggests, is the birthplace of Parmigiano Reggiano and Prosciutto di Parma. Emilia-Romagna's cuisine is also known for its rich ragù, truffles and chestnuts, and the region boasts numerous DOP-certified products that continue to feature in both traditional and modern cooking.

For pasta lovers, Emilia-Romagna offers an exceptional repertoire of regional shapes to try, including tortellini, lasagne, tagliatelle, strozzapreti, garganelli, gramigna, spoja lorda and passatelli.

TORTELLINI

The exact origins of this classic pasta shape are unknown, with both Modena and Bologna claiming it as their own. The first recorded reference appears in 1570, within a recipe by Bartolomeo Scappi in which he named the shape 'tortelletti'. However, the name may have been used much earlier than Bartolomeo's recipe, with one record suggesting this classic shape has been made as long ago as the 1300s.

There's a legend to the creation of this shape, based on the 1622 poem *La Secchia Rapita* (*The Stolen Bucket*) by Alessandro Tassoni. Following a battle between Modena and Bologna, the gods Venus, Bacchus and Mars stayed at an inn in the town of Castelfranco Emilia, and the innkeeper, mesmerised by Venus' navel, was inspired to create the tortellini shape in its likeness. The poem was intended to symbolically bridge the gap between Modena and Bologna, using their beloved tortellini and Castelfranco Emilia, which lay between the two towns.

Bologna and Modena each has its own preferred tortellini style: Bologna's tortellini is slightly smaller and uses raw meat such as mortadella, while Modena's is slightly larger and filled with cooked meat.

In 1974, to end the tortellini origin controversy between the two cities, the Academia Italiana della Cucina (Italian Academy of Cookery) and the Confraternita del Tortellino registered and deposited the true and authentic ingredients of tortellini with the Bologna Chamber of Commerce. However, even with this registration, families and towns still vary ingredients and quantities.

Tortellini in brodo

TORTELLINI IN BROTH

✶
Serves
6
✶

Brodo is the most common and authentic way to serve tortellini. A childhood memory of mine is my mum making brodo every Saturday – the aroma of the delicious broth simmering away on our stovetop is still vivid. It's a tradition that continues in my own kitchen today, whenever I feel the need for comfort.

I've included two fillings: one traditional in my family, and the other a modern vegetarian version using mushrooms. Yes, I may attract monumental criticism, but I've served the mushroom filling to friends and in a couple of my cooking classes, and the verdict was positive – in fact delicious. Some even thought it was a meat filling!

The pasta dough can be made using a mix of 00 flour and fine semolina flour, as I have called for here, or a simple egg dough (see page 17).

Pasta tools

pasta machine or rolling pin
pasta cutter

Brodo

1 whole chicken (about 1.5 kg/ 3 lb 5 oz) jointed into 8 pieces, or 4 leg quarters, or 8–10 large drumsticks
1–2 beef stock bones or 1 osso buco piece (optional)
1 onion, halved
2 carrots, halved
2 celery stalks, cut in 2–3 pieces
2 bay leaves
1 tablespoon salt
3–4 parsley sprigs
1 tomato, halved (optional)
1 Parmigiano Reggiano rind

Fillings

Mushroom and ricotta filling

40 ml (1¼ fl oz) extra virgin olive oil
1 onion, finely chopped
200 g (7 oz) mushrooms, finely chopped
300 g (10½ oz) ricotta, drained
1 egg (about 55 g/2 oz), lightly beaten

For the brodo

Place all the ingredients except the parmigiano rind in a large heavy-based stockpot, cover with cold water and bring to the boil. Reduce the heat to low, cover and simmer for 1½ hours, skimming every 30 minutes.

Add the parmigiano rind and continue simmering for a further 1½ hours, skimming occasionally. Taste and season as needed.

After 3 hours, remove the chicken and vegetables, then strain the liquid through a fine sieve into a clean pot. With a spoon or a ladle, press down on the solids to extract any the remaining liquid (which contains plenty of flavour!).

If not using immediately, cool, cover and refrigerate the stock for up to 5 days. Remove the fat layer before reheating.

For the filling

For the mushroom and ricotta filling, heat the olive oil in a frying pan over medium heat. Saute the onion until soft, then add the mushrooms and cook until softened and slightly browned. Set aside to cool.

In a bowl, combine the cooled mixture with the ricotta and egg. Season to taste with salt and pepper and set aside.

For the traditional meat filling, combine all the ingredients in a bowl and mix well. Set aside.

For the pasta

Mix, knead and rest the pasta ingredients following the instructions on pages 17–18. Place the rested dough on a work surface that has been lightly dusted with 00 flour and divide into four portions. Cover the portions so they don't dry out.

Traditional meat filling
100 g (3½ oz) minced (ground) pork loin
150 g (5½ oz) mortadella, finely chopped
150 g (5½ oz) prosciutto, finely chopped
100 g (3½ oz) Parmigiano Reggiano, finely grated
1 egg (about 55 g/2 oz), lightly beaten

Pasta
300 g (2 cups) 00 flour, plus extra for dusting
100 g (3½ oz) fine semolina flour, plus extra for dusting
3 eggs (about 165 g/6 oz total), plus 3 egg yolks
pinch of salt

To serve
grated Parmigiano Reggiano

Working with one portion at a time, roll the dough into sheets using a pasta machine (see pages 18–21) or by hand (pages 21–22). Roll the pasta sheet to a thickness of 2 mm (approx. 1/16 in). Depending on your pasta machine, this may be setting 5 or 6.

To form the tortellini
Place the pasta sheet back on your lightly floured work surface and cut into 4–5 cm (1¾–2 in) squares with a pasta cutter.

Spoon or pipe a scant teaspoon of filling into the centre of each square. Work in batches (around 10 tortellini at a time) and keep the remaining dough covered to prevent it drying out.

Carefully fold one corner over the filling to form a triangle. Press gently around the filling to remove any air and seal the edges well.

Bring the two outer points together, curve them around your fingertip under the 'belly' of the tortellini and overlap to enclose. Press firmly so the join is even and not too thick. We are aiming for an evenly joined dough, as this will help the tortellini to cook evenly. Repeat this process until all the tortellini are made.

Place the tortellini onto a tray that has been lightly dusted with fine semolina flour. Repeat the rolling, cutting and filling process with the remaining dough portions and filling, then set aside until ready to cook.

To cook the tortellini and serve
When ready to serve, bring the brodo to the boil and gently add the tortellini, slowly stirring a few times. Cook for about 3–4 minutes, until al dente, or until they float to the surface.

Turn off the heat and cover the pot to let the tortellini rest for a couple of minutes so they absorb the silky, gorgeous brodo.

Serve the tortellini in bowls with hot brodo, topped with grated parmigiano.

Notes
When making brodo, always cover your ingredients with cold water before cooking – this will ensure your brodo is clear and not cloudy.

Store the brodo in an airtight container for 4–5 days in the fridge or 3 months in the freezer.

Any leftover pasta squares can be shaped into sorpresine (little surprises) – unfilled tortellini twists (page 120).

Tortellini in brodo ✶ *Tortellini in broth*

Sorpresine in brodo

UNFILLED TORTELLINI IN BROTH

✶
Serves
1
✶

This is a great way to make the most of any leftover pasta and brodo (broth) when making tortellini (page 116), although they would be equally as delicious served in a light tomato sugo (sauce), mixed with a touch of mascarpone.

leftover tortellini pasta dough (page 116), rolled into sheets
fine semolina flour, for dusting

To serve
500 ml (2 cups) leftover Brodo (page 116), warmed
grated Parmigiano Reggiano

For the pasta
Cut the pasta sheet into 4 cm (1½ in) squares.

Working with one square at a time, bring the two opposite points together and pinch to seal.

Use your finger to gently push in the middle of the folded edge. This will force the two shorter sides to bend back, which will make the next fold a little easier.

Take the two remaining non-pinched ends, bring them together and pinch to seal.

Place the sorpresine onto a tray that has been lightly dusted with fine semolina flour. Repeat the cutting and shaping process with the remaining dough portions, then set aside until ready to cook.

To cook the sorpresine and serve
Bring the brodo to the boil and gently add the sorpresine, slowly stirring a few times. Cook for about 3–4 minutes, until al dente, or until they float to the surface.

Serve the sorpresine in a bowl with plenty of hot brodo, and top with grated parmigiano.

SORPRESINE

'Sorpresine' means 'little surprises'. It is an unfilled type of tortellini that uses an egg-based dough. Sorpresine is perfect to add into brodo (broth), as the luscious liquid pools inside, and it's also a good way to use up any leftover tortellini pasta squares if your filling has run out!

The name also suggests that sorpresine was once made by families who couldn't afford the rich, meaty filling of tortellini.

STROZZAPRETI

Strozzapreti has a slightly morbid name — it translates to 'priest-strangler' — although the origin story behind it is not as dark. Dating back to the 17th century, legend has it that villagers would serve priests generous portions of this delicious pasta, which the priests devoured so quickly they were thought to risk choking. The nickname may also have carried a touch of local resentment, as priests collected taxes and were often viewed as greedy by villagers.

Strozzapreti uses an eggless dough with an approximate 50:50 ratio of flour to water, although some variations use a combination of 00 flour and semolina flour (around a 70:30 ratio). The result is a chewy, rustic pasta that holds sauce beautifully.

Strozzapreti in sugo

STROZZAPRETI IN SAUCE

*
Serves 6
*

Strozzapreti is a very easy shape to create, and once you find your rhythm, you can make large quantities quickly by twisting and tearing palm-length pieces of dough.

Pasta tools
rolling pin

Pasta
500 g (1 lb 2 oz) fine semolina flour, plus extra for dusting
250 ml (1 cup) water
pinch of salt

Sauce
80 ml (⅓ cup) extra virgin olive oil, or as needed
3 garlic cloves, finely chopped
1.5 kg (3 lb 5 oz) passata (pureed tomatoes)
small bunch of basil, plus extra leaves to serve

To serve
grated Parmigiano Reggiano

For the pasta

Mix, knead and rest the pasta ingredients following the instructions on pages 17–18. Place the rested dough on a work surface that has been lightly dusted with fine semolina flour and divide into two portions. Cover the portions so they don't dry out.

Working with one portion at a time, use a rolling pin to roll the dough into a large rectangular pasta sheet about 2 mm (approx. 1/16 in) thick.

Slice the pasta sheet into long strips about 1.5 cm (½ in) wide.

Working with one strip at a time, gently stretch the strip and, starting from one end, roll and twist the dough between your palms in one smooth motion. Once the dough has twisted, tear off a piece about the length of your palm (7–8 cm/2¾–3¼ in).

Continue along the length of the strip and transfer the shaped strozzapreti onto a tray that has been lightly dusted with fine semolina flour. Repeat the rolling, cutting and shaping process with the remaining dough portions, then set aside until ready to cook.

For the sauce

In a large saucepan over medium heat, add the olive oil and garlic and saute until softened but not browned. Add the passata and stir to combine. Tear in the basil leaves and add the stalks for extra flavour. Season to taste with salt and pepper. Bring to the boil, then reduce to a simmer. For a lighter sauce, cook for 15–20 minutes; for a richer, heartier sauce, simmer for 45–60 minutes.

To cook the strozzapreti and serve

Bring a large saucepan of water to the boil over high heat, then add cooking salt. Cook the strozzapreti for 4–5 minutes, until al dente.

Use a handled colander to transfer the cooked pasta directly into the sauce and stir to coat well, adding a little pasta water if needed for extra creaminess.

Serve immediately, topped with grated parmigiano and basil leaves.

Tagliatelle al ragu

TAGLIATELLE IN MEAT SAUCE

✶
Serves
6
✶

This ribbon-shaped pasta is the perfect match for heavier sauces and, traditionally, it's served with ragu alla bolognese – a rich meat sauce. The region strictly observes this pairing and spaghetti is absolutely never used as a substitute in this perfect union!

Pasta tools

pasta machine with tagliatelle attachment or rolling pin and pasta knife

Ragu

120 ml (4 fl oz) extra virgin olive oil
150 g (5½ oz) pancetta, finely chopped
soffritto mix (1 onion, 2 carrots and 2 celery stalks, all finely diced; onion kept separate)
800 g (1 lb 12 oz) minced (ground) beef
150 ml (5 fl oz) dry red or white wine
250 ml (1 cup) beef stock, plus extra as needed
400 g (14 oz) tinned polpa (crushed) or tinned whole peeled tomatoes
2 tablespoons tomato paste (concentrated puree)
100 ml (3½ fl oz) full-cream (whole) milk

Pasta (see Note)

600 g (4 cups) 00 flour, plus extra for dusting
6 eggs (about 330 g/ 11½ oz total)
pinch of salt
fine semolina flour, for dusting

To serve

grated Parmigiano Reggiano

For the ragu

In a heavy, deep frying pan over medium heat, add 40 ml (1¼ fl oz) of the olive oil and the pancetta. Saute for 3–4 minutes. Add the onion and cook for 3 minutes, until slightly softened, then add the remaining soffritto mix of carrots and celery with the remaining olive oil. Cook for 4–5 minutes, or until softened.

Increase the heat and add the minced beef. Stir continuously until browned and any clumps break apart, allowing the liquid to evaporate.

Add the wine and stir to deglaze the base and sides of the pan. Cook for 10–15 minutes to allow the alcohol to evaporate.

Add the stock, crushed tomato and tomato paste and season to taste with salt and pepper. Mix well to combine.

Reduce the heat to medium-low, partially cover and simmer for 45 minutes, stirring occasionally.

Taste and season if needed, then stir in the milk. Add a little extra stock if the ragu is looking dry.

Simmer for a further 2–3 hours, stirring occasionally and adding stock as required. The longer you simmer, the richer the ragu becomes – aim for at least 2 hours, though 3 hours is ideal.

For the pasta

Mix, knead and rest the pasta ingredients (excluding the semolina flour) following the instructions on pages 17–18. Place the rested dough on a work surface that has been lightly dusted with 00 flour and divide into four portions. Cover the portions so they don't dry out.

Working with one portion at a time, roll the dough into sheets using a pasta machine (see pages 18–21) or by hand (pages 21–22). Roll the pasta sheet to a thickness of 1.5 mm (1/16 in). Depending on your pasta machine, this may be setting 6 or 7.

Let the pasta sheets rest on the work surface for a few minutes to slightly dry before cutting. Lightly dust a tray with fine semolina flour or have your pasta drying rack nearby. ➥

If using a pasta machine to cut the tagliatelle, fit the tagliatelle attachment to your pasta machine. Pass the pasta sheet through the attachment, gently picking up the cut strands and laying them onto the tray or rack. Repeat this process for the remaining pasta sheets, then set aside until ready to cook.

If cutting the tagliatelle by hand, lay the pasta sheet on the work surface with the short edge facing you. Lightly dust the pasta sheet with fine semolina flour and fold the pasta sheet loosely a few times along the entire length of the sheet, so you have a folded tube of dough with many layers. Gently flatten the tube, then cut the dough into strips 6 mm (¼ in) wide with a knife. Unroll the strips and lay them onto the tray or rack. Repeat this process for the remaining pasta sheets, then set aside until ready to cook.

To cook the tagliatelle and serve

Place a large saucepan of water over high heat and bring to the boil, then add cooking salt. Add the tagliatelle and cook for 4–5 minutes, or until al dente. Use a handled colander to transfer the cooked pasta directly into the ragu and toss to combine.

Top with grated parmigiano and serve immediately.

Note

You can use dried tagliatelle pasta instead of fresh if you prefer. You'll need about 500 g (1 lb 2 oz) for this recipe. Cook according to the packet instructions.

TAGLIATELLE

Tagliatelle is believed to have originated in Bologna around the 15th century. The name is derived from the Italian word 'tagliare', meaning 'to cut', which is exactly how this pasta is created — long, ribbon-like flat strips cut into 6 mm (¼ in) widths.

This pasta also has a romantic legend: in 1487, Chef Mastro Zefirano, the court cook of Giovanni II Bentivoglio of the House of Borgia, was asked to prepare a banquet to honour Lucrezia Borgia, who was passing through the city to marry her first husband, Duke Alfonso I d'Este. Inspired by her long blonde hair, Chef Zefirano created the tagliatelle shape in its likeness.

Tagliatelle

SPOJA LORDA

'Spoja lorda' (or 'sfoglia lorda') means 'dirty pasta sheet'. The pasta was traditionally made using leftover sfoglia (pasta sheets) after preparing filled pasta. A ricotta filling is lightly spread or scraped over one sheet of pasta, then covered with another sheet and cut into small squares so that they look like little tiles. This process can seem precarious — and have you thinking they couldn't possibly hold together when cooked — but miraculously, they do! If in doubt, a little extra egg helps the sheets bind together. A mix of cheeses such as stracchino, ricotta, squacquerone and parmigiano will also hold together when cooked.

I love a good food festival, and there's a Festa della Spoja Lorda held annually in April in Brisighella, the town where the pasta originated, along with the nearby town of Faenza.

Spoja lorda in brodo

SPOJA LORDA IN BROTH

✶
Serves 6
✶

Spoja lorda is usually served in winter in a glorious brodo (broth) – a bowl of exquisite and simple comfort food.

Pasta tools

pasta machine or rolling pin
smooth or fluted pasta cutter

Pasta

400 g (14 oz) 00 flour, plus extra for dusting
4 eggs (about 220 g/8 oz total)
pinch of salt
fine semolina flour, for dusting (optional)

Filling

200 g (7 oz) ricotta, drained
100 g (3½ oz) Parmigiano Reggiano or squacquerone
1 egg (about 55 g/2 oz), lightly beaten
pinch of salt
½ teaspoon ground nutmeg (optional)

To serve

1.5 litres (6 cups) Brodo (page 116)
grated Parmigiano Reggiano

For the pasta

Mix, knead and rest the pasta ingredients (excluding the semolina flour) following the instructions on pages 17–18. Place the rested dough on a work surface that has been lightly dusted with 00 flour and divide into four portions. Cover the portions so they don't dry out.

Working with one portion at a time, roll the dough into sheets using a pasta machine (see pages 18–21) or by hand (pages 21–22). Roll the pasta sheet to a thickness of 2 mm (approx. 1⁄16 in). Depending on your pasta machine, this may be setting 5 or 6.

To make the filling and form the spoja lorda

In a bowl, combine the filling ingredients. Spread a thin layer of the filling over half of one pasta sheet, then fold the other half over to cover the filling.

Gently press down to remove any air bubbles and seal the layers together. Trim the edges so the sheet has clean, even sides.

Use a smooth or fluted pasta cutter to slice the sheet into long strips about 2 cm (¾ in) wide, then cut across to create small squares.

Place the spoja lorda onto a tray that has been lightly dusted with fine semolina flour. Repeat the rolling, filling and cutting process with the remaining dough portions and filling, then set aside for at least 20–30 minutes to dry before cooking.

To cook the spoja lorda and serve

In a stockpot over high heat, bring the brodo to the boil, then reduce the heat to medium. Add the spoja lorda and cook for 3–4 minutes, until al dente.

Serve hot, topped with grated parmigiano.

Garganelli con prosciutto e piselli

GARGANELLI WITH PROSCIUTTO AND PEAS

✳
Serves 6
✳

Garganelli is traditionally served with a hearty meat or salsiccia (sausage) ragu, or with prosciutto or pancetta and piselli (peas). My version of this recipe uses prosciutto, which pairs well with butter and peas. To be honest, I love both prosciutto and pancetta and can never decide which to add – I tend to alternate between the two when I make garganelli at home.

Pasta tools

- pasta machine or rolling pin
- smooth or fluted pasta cutter
- garganelli board or pettine (see page 136)
- small wooden dowel, 8–10 mm (approx. ¼ in) in diameter

Pasta

- 400 g (14 oz) 00 flour, plus extra for dusting
- 4 eggs (about 220 g/ 8 oz total)
- pinch of salt
- fine semolina flour, for dusting

Sauce

- 100–120 ml (3½–4 fl oz) extra virgin olive oil, or as needed
- 1 onion, halved and thinly sliced
- pinch salt
- 25 g (1 oz) unsalted butter
- 125 g (4½ oz) frozen or fresh peas (shelled)
- 100 g (3½ oz) prosciutto or pancetta, sliced into short batons

To serve

- grated Parmigiano Reggiano

For the pasta

Mix, knead and rest the pasta ingredients (excluding the semolina flour) following the instructions on pages 17–18. Place the rested dough on a work surface that has been lightly dusted with 00 flour and divide into four portions. Cover the portions so they don't dry out.

Working with one portion at a time, roll the dough into sheets using a pasta machine (see pages 18–21) or by hand (pages 21–22). Roll the pasta sheet to a thickness of 2 mm (approx. $\frac{1}{16}$ in). Depending on your pasta machine, this may be setting 5 or 6.

Use a pasta cutter to slice the sheet into long strips about 4 cm (1½ in) wide, then cut across to create squares.

To shape the garganelli, place one pasta square diagonally on a garganelli board. Using the small wooden dowel, roll the pasta square over the board to create a sealed tube with ridges. Roll back and forth to secure the seam and form ridges all around the pasta.

Place the garganelli onto a tray that has been lightly dusted with fine semolina flour. Repeat the rolling, cutting and shaping process with the remaining dough portions, then set aside until ready to cook.

For the sauce

In a large frying pan over medium heat, add the olive oil and onion. Add the salt and cook for 5 minutes, or until the onion has softened and begun to break down.

Add the butter, then the peas, and cook for 5 minutes.

Stir in the prosciutto and cook for a further 2–3 minutes. Taste and season with salt and pepper as needed. Reduce the heat to low until the pasta is ready to join the sauce. ➥

To cook the garganelli and serve

While the sauce is simmering, bring a large saucepan of water to the boil over high heat, then add cooking salt. Add the garganelli and cook for 4–5 minutes, or until al dente.

Use a handled colander to transfer the cooked pasta directly into the sauce. Toss gently to coat, adding some pasta water into the sauce if needed for creaminess.

Serve immediately, topped with grated parmigiano.

GARGANELLI

Garganelli dates back to around 1725, though, like many pasta shapes, it was likely made long before then. The dialect name 'garganel' translates to 'chicken gullet', referencing the pasta's tubular shape and ridged texture.

There are several legends about the origin of this pasta shape. One tells of a cook preparing cappelletti (a type of filled pasta) in the home of Cardinal Cornelio Bentivoglio d'Aragona, only to discover that the prepared filling had been eaten by a kitchen cat. Thinking quickly, the cook rolled the leftover pasta squares into tubes using a weaving loom or pettine (comb) tool, which indented ridges along the surface. Once rolled, the garganelli shape has pointed ends that resemble a quill.

The delicate pettine has since become a common pasta tool, and today you can still buy either the traditional wooden pettine or a sturdier version known as a garganelli board.

Firenze
MARCHE
Ancona
TOSCANA
Perugia
UMBRIA
Pescara
ABRUZZO
Roma
LAZIO

PART TWO

CENTRAL

Central Italy comprises five regions — Toscana, Umbria, Marche, Lazio and Abruzzo — the majority of which were under the direct control of the Pope and the Catholic Church from the 8th century until the unification of Italy in the 1800s. Home to key historical cities such as Rome, Florence, Assisi and Siena, Central Italy has a rich political, religious, cultural and culinary history. Alongside iconic landmarks including the Leaning Tower of Pisa, the Colosseum and the Vatican, you'll find regional specialties and rustic dishes that emphasise the traditional cucina povera (peasant cooking) style of cooking. Expect seasonal, local ingredients such as olive oil, herbs, meat, truffles and tomatoes, as well as time-honoured cooking methods. Sandwiched between the Adriatic Sea to the east and the Tyrrhenian Sea to the west, Central Italy is known for its fertile soil and a climate that is well suited to farming and the cultivation of farro, saffron and chestnuts.

PAPPARDELLE
(page 144)

PICI
(page 147)

TOSCANA

Toscana, or Tuscany, with its landscape that is dotted with cypress trees and coastline along the Tyrrhenian Sea draws many tourists each year. Toscana is regarded as the birthplace of the Renaissance, and its capital, Florence, is home to some of the most recognisable Renaissance art and architecture in the world. The Cathedral of Santa Maria del Fiore is a creative masterpiece of Renaissance architecture; the Uffizi Gallery, which features many of Botticelli's works; the Ponte Vecchio, the medieval stone bridge that spans the Arno River; and Michelangelo's statue of David in the Galleria dell'Accademia can all be found here.

In Toscana, you'll also find Pisa and its famous Leaning Tower, which was already leaning upon its completion in 1372. There's also Lucca, a well-preserved medieval city encircled by Renaissance-era walls that date back to the 16th century. This picturesque city features charming cobblestone streets, a medieval clock tower and the museum Casa di Puccini, which is housed in the building that the great opera composer Giacomo Puccini was born in in 1858.

The region's flair for artistry is reflected in Tuscan cuisine, which is deceptively simple, allowing flavours to shine. Dishes rely on local, seasonal ingredients such as olive oil, vegetables, beans and meat. For food on the go, Florentines serve lampredotto, a traditional street-food sandwich made from the fourth stomach of a cow — not for the faint-hearted! Another meaty favourite is bistecca alla Fiorentina, Florence's signature dish. This generous T-bone steak is large enough to share between two to three people.

When it comes to pasta, Toscana is known for pappardelle, pici and pasta e ceci, a hearty soup made with pasta and chickpeas (garbanzo beans).

Pappardelle alla boscaiola

✶
Serves
4
✶

One of my favourite ways to serve pappardelle is alla boscaiola, a rustic-style pasta dish which translates to 'woodsman-style'. This dish should include porcini, which is a common foraged mushroom in the neighbouring regions of Toscana and Emilia-Romagna. I've included two equally delicious options: a bianco version with cream (pictured), and a rosso version with tomatoes.

Pasta tools

pasta machine or rolling pin
pasta knife

Pasta (see Notes)

400 g (14 oz) 00 flour, plus extra for dusting
4 eggs (about 220 g/ 8 oz total)
pinch of salt
fine semolina flour, for dusting

Sauce

5 Italian pork sausages, casings removed and filling crumbled into pieces
100 ml (3½ fl oz) extra virgin olive oil, or as needed
1 onion, finely chopped
500 g (1 lb 2 oz) mixed mushrooms, sliced (including porcini; see Note)
125 ml (½ cup) dry white wine
handful of parsley, chopped

For bianco version

300 ml (10 fl oz) cream

For rosso version

400 g (14 oz) tinned whole peeled tomatoes

To serve

grated Parmigiano Reggiano

For the pasta

Mix, knead and rest the pasta ingredients (excluding the semolina flour) following the instructions on pages 17–18. Place the rested dough on a work surface that has been lightly dusted with 00 flour and divide into four portions. Cover the portions so they don't dry out.

Working with one portion at a time, roll the dough into sheets using a pasta machine (see pages 18–21) or by hand (pages 21–22). Roll the pasta sheet to a thickness of 2 mm (approx. $\frac{1}{16}$ in). Depending on your pasta machine, this may be between settings 5 and 6.

Lay the pasta sheet on the work surface with the short edge facing you. Lightly dust the pasta sheet with fine semolina flour and fold the pasta sheet loosely a few times along the entire length of the sheet, so you have a folded tube of dough with many layers. Gently flatten the tube, then cut the dough into strips 2.5–4 cm (1–1½ in) wide with a knife. Unroll the strips and place the pappardelle onto a tray or a pasta drying rack that has been lightly dusted with fine semolina flour. Repeat the rolling and cutting process with the remaining dough portions, then set aside until ready to cook.

For the sauce

Cook the sausages in a dry large, heavy-based frying pan over medium heat until browned, then remove and set aside.

In the same pan, add the olive oil and onion, and saute until softened but not browned.

Add the mushrooms and cook until lightly browned.

Return the sausages to the pan, pour in the wine and cook until almost evaporated. Add half of the chopped parsley and stir through. ➥

For the bianco version, add the cream and cook for 5 minutes, seasoning to taste.

For the rosso version, crush the tinned tomatoes, either by hand or with a fork. Add them to the pan and simmer for 20 minutes, seasoning to taste.

Reduce the heat to low and keep warm until the pasta is ready to be added.

To cook the pappardelle and serve

Bring a large saucepan of water to the boil over high heat, then add cooking salt. Cook the pappardelle for 4–5 minutes, or until al dente.

Use a handled colander to transfer the cooked pasta directly into the sauce, add the remaining parsley and toss until well coated.

Top with grated parmigiano and serve immediately.

Notes

You can use dried pappardelle instead of fresh if you prefer. You'll need about 500 g (1 lb 2 oz) for this recipe. Cook according to the packet instructions.

For the 500 g (1 lb 2 oz) mushroom mix, aim for at least three varieties, one of which should be porcini for its rich, earthy depth. I would suggest using no more than 100 g (3½ oz) fresh porcini. If fresh is unavailable, rehydrate 10 g (¼ oz) dried porcini in warm water for 15 minutes. For added flavour, you can also strain the soaking liquid and add it to the sauce.

PAPPARDELLE

Pappardelle dates back to the 14th century in the central regions of Toscana. The name derives from the Italian verb 'pappare', meaning 'to eat'. It was traditionally made with eggs and 00 flour, but some versions also used chestnut flour, which was readily available in the region.

Pappardelle is a wide, flat pasta, similar to fettuccine but broader, typically anywhere between 2.5–4 cm (1–1½ in). Its slightly rough texture and exaggerated width pairs perfectly with richer sugos and ragus (sauces and meat-based sauces) – it is common to see pappardelle stirred through a wild boar ragu or a hearty mushroom ragu.

Pici all'aglione

PICI WITH GARLIC SAUCE

✳
Serves
4
✳

I love the rustic shape of pici and its chewy texture. This dish uses large, mild, sweet garlic – a specialty grown in the Val di Chiana area. When sourcing from your local market, look for large, delicate varieties such as elephant garlic.

Traditionally all'aglione includes tomatoes, but I've omitted them here to really hero the aromatic element of the chilli and the garlic. Cheese is not usually added when serving this traditional dish.

Pasta tools

rolling pin

Pasta

400 g (14 oz) 00 flour, plus extra for dusting
200 ml (7 fl oz) water
20 ml (¾ fl oz) extra virgin olive oil
pinch of salt
fine semolina flour, for dusting

Sauce

90 ml (3 fl oz) extra virgin olive oil
6 garlic cloves, crushed
1 small red chilli, chopped

For the pasta

Mix, knead and rest the pasta ingredients (excluding the semolina flour) following the instructions on pages 17–18.

Place the rested dough onto a work surface that has been dusted with fine semolina flour. Using a rolling pin, roll the pasta sheet to a thickness of 5 mm (approx. ¼ in).

Cut long strips from the pasta sheet, approximately 5-8 mm (approx. ¼ in) wide. Working with one strip at a time, hand-roll each strip using both hands. Start in the centre and work towards the ends, stretching the dough slightly as you roll to form very long pici strands. They may all look irregular but that's the beauty of this pasta!

Place the pici onto a tray that has been lightly dusted with fine semolina flour. Repeat the rolling and shaping process with the remaining dough, then set aside until ready to cook.

To cook the pici and the sauce

Bring a large saucepan of water to the boil over high heat, then add cooking salt. Cook the pici for 4–5 minutes, or until al dente.

Meanwhile, in a large frying pan over medium heat, add the olive oil and garlic and cook for 3 minutes, until softened but not browned.

Add the chilli and saute for 2 minutes.

Use a handled colander to transfer the cooked pici directly into the sauce and toss well to coat, adding a little pasta water to the sauce for extra creaminess. Season to taste with salt before serving.

Serve immediately and savour the delicate flavour of this classic Tuscan dish!

PICI

Pici is an ancient pasta shape that traces back to the Etruscans, possibly as early as the 5th century CE. It is a long, thick, irregular spaghetti-style pasta from Siena and Val di Chiana. It goes by many other names — pinci, lunghetti, filarelli, ceriole and strangozzi. The name 'pici' is derived from the local word 'appicciare', meaning 'to stick'.

What is served with pici varies from village to village: some prepare it with a duck ragu, all'etrusca (pici served in a pesto made from hard boiled eggs, typically served with asparagus), or in salsa all'aglione, as I have prepared here.

MACCHERONCINI DI CAMPOFILONE (page 152)

VINCISGRASSI (page 154)

PASSATELLI (page 156)

MARCHE

Marche, also known as Le Marche, is located along the Adriatic coastline, with the port city of Ancona as its capital. Stretching from the coast to the Apennine Mountains, Marche is characterised by medieval hilltop towns, tiny coastal villages and cities adorned with palaces from the Renaissance era.

Pesaro is a coastal town on the Adriatic coast and a destination for music lovers. Being hometown of the great composer Gioachino Rossini, it has been designated a UNESCO Creative City of Music. Wander through the historic main square, Piazza del Popolo, which is notable for its fountain, La Pupilla di Pesaro, and the Palazzo Ducale, or stroll along the beautiful seafront promenade that stretches for over 7 kilometres (4.3 miles) of inviting sandy beaches.

Marche cuisine is known for its seafood, as well as its farmed and foraged ingredients. The region also aligns closely with the principles of the Slow Food movement, with a strong focus on local and seasonal produce. Marche is renowned for its truffles, olive all'ascolana (filled, coated and fried olives), verdure fritte (fried vegetables), crema fritta (fried custard), prosciutto, ciauscolo (a spreadable Italian salami), and cheeses such as pecorino, caciotta and fossa. Pasta specialties include vincisgrassi, a lasagne-style dish, and ricotta calcioni, a fried ravioli-style dish. If you're looking for a wine to pair with your pasta, Marche is also home to the renowned Verdicchio.

Maccheroncini di Campofilone con Marchigiano ragu

✳
Serves
4
✳

Maccheroncini de Camofilone is an exceptionally thin pasta (see page 152), which can be tricky to master at home. I've adapted the measurements in the recipe below so it's a little easier to form these beautiful, thin strands at home.

This ragu, which is typical of the Marche region, uses a blend of minced beef and pork, but you can also add minced chicken if you prefer.

Pasta tools

pasta machine or rolling pin
pasta knife

Ragu

80 ml (⅓ cup) extra virgin olive oil
soffritto mix (1 onion, 1 carrot and 1 celery stalk, all finely diced)
200 g (7 oz) minced (ground) beef
200 g (7 oz) minced (ground) pork
1 × 200–300 g (7–10½ oz) beef marrow bone
100 ml (3½ fl oz) dry white wine (such as Verdicchio or Passerina)
handful of parsley, chopped
handful of oregano leaves, chopped
handful of sage leaves, chopped
750 g (1 lb 11 oz) passata (pureed tomatoes)

Pasta (see Note)

400 g (14 oz) 00 flour, plus extra for dusting
4 eggs (about 220 g/8 oz total)
pinch of salt
fine semolina flour, for dusting

For the ragu

In a large, heavy-based saucepan, heat the olive oil over medium heat. Add the soffritto mix and cook until softened, about 8 minutes.

Add the minced beef, pork, marrow bone, white wine, parsley, oregano and sage. Stir well to combine and cook until the wine has evaporated and the meat has slightly browned.

Add the passata, season with salt and pepper, and reduce the heat to low. Simmer for 1½–2 hours, stirring occasionally, until the ragu is gloriously luscious.

For the pasta

Mix, knead and rest the pasta ingredients (excluding the semolina flour) following the instructions on pages 17–18. Place the rested dough on a work surface that has been lightly dusted with 00 flour and divide into four portions. Cover the portions so they don't dry out.

Working with one portion at a time, roll the dough into sheets using a pasta machine (see pages 18–21) or by hand (pages 21–22). Roll the pasta sheet to a thickness of 1.5 mm (1/16 in). Depending on your pasta machine, this may be setting 6 or 7.

Lay the pasta sheet on the work surface with the short edge facing you. Lightly dust the pasta sheet with fine semolina flour and fold the pasta sheet loosely a few times along the entire length of the sheet, so you have a folded tube of dough with many layers. Gently flatten the tube, then cut the dough into strips 1.5 mm (1/16 in) wide with a knife. Unroll the strips and place the cut strands onto a tray or a pasta drying rack that has been lightly dusted with fine semolina flour. Repeat the rolling and cutting process with the remaining dough portions, then set aside until ready to cook. ➥

To serve
grated Pecorino Romano

To cook the maccheroncini and serve
Bring a large saucepan of water to the boil over high heat, then add cooking salt. Cook the maccheroncini for 4–5 minutes, until al dente.

Meanwhile, return the ragu to the heat, if needed. Remove the marrow bone from the ragu and taste for seasoning. Use a handled colander to transfer the cooked pasta directly into the ragu and toss until well coated.

Serve immediately, topped with grated pecorino.

Note
You can substitute dried maccheroncini, tagliolini or spaghetti for the fresh version if you prefer. You'll need about 500 g (1 lb 2 oz) for this recipe. Cook according to the packet instructions.

MACCHERONCINI DI CAMPOFILONE

Maccheroncini di Campofilone is a delicate, handmade, angel hair–style pasta from Marche. The ancient recipe for this pasta is believed to date back more than 600 years.

Each strand is only 0.8–1 mm (approx. 1/32 in) wide and 0.5–0.7 mm (barely 1/32 in) thick. These delicate strands can be between 35 and 60 cm (14 and 24 in) long. Still produced by hand today, this thin pasta cooks in just 2 minutes.

In 2013, Maccheroncini di Campofilone became the first egg pasta to receive the significant Indicazione Geografica Protetta (IGP) status. Every August, the historic centre of Campofilone hosts the Maccheroncini di Campofilone Festival, where thousands of locals and visitors gather to enjoy the pasta served in a rich ragu.

Vincisgrassi ai funghi

LAYERED BAKED PASTA WITH MIXED MUSHROOMS

✳
Serves
6–8
✳

Vincisgrassi is a baked pasta dish that is similar to lasagne but has its own flair. I'm sharing a mushroom and prosciutto cotto version here, as I'm not a huge fan of offal – the traditional filling. Some of my family may be giggling or shocked, but it's true!

Pasta tools

pasta machine or rolling pin

Pasta

300 g (2 cups) 00 flour, plus extra for dusting
150 g (5½ oz) fine semolina flour, plus extra for dusting
3 eggs (about 165 g/6 oz total)
50 g (1¾ oz) unsalted butter, softened
60 ml (¼ cup) marsala or other sweet wine

Bechamel

80 g (2¾ oz) unsalted butter
80 g (2¾ oz) plain (all-purpose) flour
800 ml (27 fl oz) full-cream (whole) milk, warmed, plus extra if needed
½ teaspoon freshly grated or ground nutmeg (optional)

Mushroom sauce

200 ml (7 fl oz) chicken stock
50 g (1¾ oz) dried or fresh porcini mushrooms
80–100 ml (2½–3½ fl oz) extra virgin olive oil
30 g (1 oz) unsalted butter
2 garlic cloves, crushed
400 g (14 oz) mixed mushrooms, sliced (I like portobello, Swiss brown and button)
3–4 thyme sprigs, leaves only
100 ml (3½ fl oz) dry white wine
handful of parsley, chopped

For the pasta

Mix, knead and rest the pasta ingredients following the instructions on pages 17–18. Place the rested dough on a work surface that has been lightly dusted with 00 flour and divide into four portions. Cover the portions so they don't dry out.

Working with one portion at a time, roll the dough into sheets using a pasta machine (see pages 18–21) or by hand (pages 21–22). Roll the pasta sheet to a thickness of 2 mm (approx. 1⁄16 in). Depending on your pasta machine, this may be setting 5 or 6. Repeat with the remaining portions of dough.

Cut the pasta sheets to fit your oven dish. Lightly dust each cut sheet with fine semolina flour before setting aside until ready to cook. Take care not to overlap the cut pasta sheets to avoid them sticking together.

For the bechamel

Melt the butter in a large saucepan over medium heat. Add the flour and whisk until well incorporated. Gradually add the warm milk, whisking constantly, until the sauce thickens. If it becomes too thick, add a little extra milk. Add the nutmeg, if using, and season to taste with salt and pepper.

For the mushroom sauce

If using dried porcini, bring the chicken stock to the boil in a small saucepan, then remove from heat. Add the dried porcini and soak for 20–30 minutes. Drain, chop and set aside, reserving the chicken stock to use later – it will be infused with the delicious porcini flavour.

If using fresh porcini, chop the porcini mushrooms and set aside.

In a large saucepan over medium heat, add the olive oil, butter and garlic, and cook until the garlic has softened but not browned.

Add the porcini along with the remaining mushrooms and thyme to the saucepan and saute for a few minutes until lightly browned. Pour in the wine and cook until almost evaporated, then add the chicken stock. Simmer for 8–10 minutes, until the sauce has slightly reduced. ➥

VINCISGRASSI

The story goes that vincisgrassi was created in 1799 in Ancona for a dinner honouring the Austrian general, Prince of Windischgrätz, whose name inspired the dish. The recipe included extra luxurious ingredients that impressed the general — and the dish lives on today.

As with many Italian legends, its origins are debated. In 1779, a similar recipe called Princisgras appeared in *Il Cuoco Maceratese* (*The Cook of Macerata*) by Antonio Nebbia. That version included truffle, mushrooms and bechamel, suggesting it may have been a more refined, aristocratic dish.

Vincisgrassi is very similar to another layered pasta dish, the much beloved lasagne. The two dishes are quite similar, but the key difference is in the sauce. While lasagne typically layers a tomato ragu between the pasta sheets, vincisgrassi is typically layered with a meat-based ragu, which may consist of offal, chicken, chicken livers, pork or beef; however, many will forgo meat entirely and use mushrooms instead. The pasta dough is traditionally made with eggs, though some versions may include butter or even marsala instead of eggs.

To assemble
200 g (7 oz) prosciutto cotto, chopped
180 g (6½ oz) Parmigiano Reggiano, grated, plus extra as needed

To serve
crusty bread

Stir in three-quarters of the bechamel, add the parsley and season to taste. Reserve the remaining bechamel for the top layer.

To assemble and bake
Preheat the oven to 200°C (400°F).

Line your bench space or table with a few tea towels. Bring a large saucepan of water to the boil over high heat, then add cooking salt. Cook your pre-cut pasta sheets for 2 minutes – this will parcook the pasta sheets. Cook the pasta sheets in batches of 1 or 2 to ensure they don't stick together when cooking. Use a handled colander to drain the pasta sheets, then lay them flat on the tea towels to dry slightly, again taking care not to let the parcooked sheets overlap, as they will stick together.

Spread a thin layer of the mushroom sauce over the base of a large rectangular ovenproof dish.

Add a layer of pasta to fit snugly, followed by more sauce, some chopped prosciutto cotto and a sprinkle of grated parmigiano.

Continue layering pasta, sauce, prosciutto cotto and parmigiano until you near the top of the dish, or until all the sauce is used.

Finish with a pasta layer, then spread over the reserved bechamel and top with a good handful of parmigiano.

Bake for 20–30 minutes, until the bechamel and parmigiano start to bubble and the top is lightly golden. It's okay if you have any pasta overhanging the edge, it will become deliciously crisp in the oven!

Allow to cool for 10 minutes before serving with some fresh, crusty bread on the side.

Passatelli in brodo

PASSATELLI IN BROTH

Serves 6

Technically, passatelli isn't a true pasta, but a cucina povera (peasant cooking) style of preparation. It's earned its place on any pasta lover's list – a rustic favourite that brings simple comfort to the table.

Pasta tools

potato ricer with large holes that are at least 5 mm (approx. ¼ in) in diameter

Pasta

- 3 eggs (about 165 g/6 oz total), lightly beaten
- 200 g (7 oz) stale, dried breadcrumbs
- 150 g (5½ oz) Parmigiano Reggiano, grated, plus extra to serve
- ½ teaspoon freshly grated nutmeg
- ½ teaspoon lemon zest
- pinch of salt
- 20–40 g (¾–1½oz) 00 flour or extra breadcrumbs, only if required

To cook

- 1.5 litres (6 cups) Brodo (page 116)

For the pasta

In a large bowl, combine all the ingredients except the 00 flour, then gently knead to form a soft, pliable dough. If the mixture feels too wet, add 1–2 tablespoons of 00 flour, or just enough so the dough holds together. Cover and rest for 20–30 minutes.

Meanwhile, place your brodo in a large saucepan and bring to the boil. Reduce to a low simmer.

To create the passatelli

To test the pasta's consistency, press a small piece of dough through the potato ricer into the simmering brodo. If the pasta breaks apart when it hits the brodo, knead a little extra 00 flour into the dough and retest. When the dough holds together in the brodo, continue to the next step.

Lay a clean tea towel on a large plate or tray. Cut off a small piece of dough and push it through the ricer. As strands start to pass through, cut them into 5–7 cm (2–2¾ in) lengths with scissors or a knife, allowing them to drop onto the prepared plate. Repeat with the remaining dough.

Transfer the passatelli into the simmering brodo and cook for 2–3 minutes, until they rise to the surface.

Ladle into bowls and top with extra grated parmigiano. Serve immediately.

PASSATELLI

Passatelli originates from both Le Marche and Emilia-Romagna. This shape is usually served in brodo (broth), though it can also be stirred through a meaty tomato sugo (sauce). The dough is made from eggs, breadcrumbs, Parmigiano Reggiano and a touch of nutmeg, and is formed by pressing the dough through a potato ricer. A common variation adds spinach to the dough mixture.

PASTA ALLA NORCINA
(page 160)
CIRIOLE
(page 163)
STRANGOZZI
(page 166)

UMBRIA

Umbria, with its stunningly lush landscape, is known as the green heart of Italy. This landlocked region receives fewer visitors than its neighbour, Toscana; however, you'll find plenty of natural wonders, as well as notable villas, churches and palaces in cities such as Orvieto, Assisi and Perugia.

Perugia, the capital city, is known for its world-famous chocolate, Il Bacio Perugina (Perugia's kiss), also known as Baci, which was invented by Luisa Spagnoli in 1922. The city also hosts the annual Eurochocolate Festival in mid-October.

Assisi is a hilltop town with deep religious significance for Christians as the birthplace and final resting place of Saint Francis, the patron saint of Italy. His tomb is housed at the Basilica di San Francesco, and nearby you can visit the Basilica di Santa Chiara, the Basilica di Santa Maria degli Angeli and the medieval fortress Rocca Maggiore, which offers breathtaking views.

Umbria has a rich agricultural heritage, which provides an array of ingredients to cook with. The cuisine remains simple and is classified as cucina povera (peasant cooking), making use of local ingredients such as olive oil, lentils, game meat, pork (often made into sausages and salumi), highly prized truffles, and spices such as cinnamon and nutmeg. The region also holds DOC (Denominazione di origine controllata) and IGP (Indicazione Geografica Protetta) status for its wines and various cured pork products.

When it comes to regional pasta dishes, you'll find fettuccine con ricotta, pasta alla Norcina (a sausage and cream sauce), strozzapreti, pappardelle alla lepre (wild hare ragu) and pappardelle alla cinghiale (wild boar ragu).

Pasta alla Norcina

*
Serves
6
*

Norcia is renowned for its pork sausages, and this dish spotlights the delicious ingredient alongside mushrooms and Umbrian wine. If you're able to source truffles, I recommend shaving some in during the final stages of cooking the sauce and again when serving. The flavour is so special!

- 80 ml (⅓ cup) extra virgin olive oil
- 1 onion, chopped
- 1 garlic clove, crushed
- 3–4 Italian pork sausages, casings removed and filling crumbled into pieces
- 200 g (7 oz) mixed mushrooms, sliced
- 150 ml (5 fl oz) dry white wine (such as Verdicchio or pinot grigio)
- 200 ml (7 fl oz) cream (35% fat)
- 1 black truffle (optional)
- 500 g (1 lb 2 oz) dried penne, rigatoni or other short pasta
- grated Pecorino Romano, to serve

Heat the oil in a large saucepan over medium heat. Add the onion and garlic and saute until softened and slightly browned.

Add the sausage and cook, breaking the pieces up with a wooden spoon, until browned.

Add the mushrooms and cook until softened and lightly browned.

Pour in the wine and let it bubble, deglazing if needed by scraping any browned bits from the pan. Cook until slightly reduced.

Stir in the cream. If using truffle, add some shavings and stir until well combined. Simmer gently for about 5 minutes. Taste and season with salt and pepper.

Bring a large saucepan of water to the boil over high heat, then add cooking salt. Cook the pasta according to the packet instructions.

Use a handled colander to transfer the cooked pasta directly into the sauce. Toss well to coat, adding a little pasta water if needed for extra creaminess.

Serve topped with grated pecorino and extra truffle, if using.

PASTA ALLA NORCINA

This dish originates from the medieval town of Norcia, famous for truffles, mushrooms (especially porcini), wild asparagus and pork from locally raised pigs. The town is especially celebrated for its cured meat products, such as salami, prosciutto and pancetta — which are easier to produce here due to the cool yet humid weather conditions.

The local butchers of the town who specialise in cured meats are called 'norcini', and their stores are known as 'norcinerie'. When you visit, ordering pasta alla Norcina is the best way to experience the town's special pork sausage.

Ciriole alla Ternana

*
Serves
4
*

Ciriole alla Ternana is a simple dish that is very popular in the Umbrian province of Terni. As ciriole are a more substantial, thicker shape of pasta compared to other long pastas, they pair especially well with a flavourful, aromatic sugo (sauce).

The simple flavours of tomato, garlic, chilli and some fresh basil are all you need to make these beautiful handmade strands of pasta sing!

Pasta tools

pasta machine or rolling pin
pasta knife

Pasta (see Note)

300 g (2 cups) 00 flour, plus extra for dusting
100 g (3½ oz) fine semolina flour, plus extra for dusting
200 ml (7 fl oz) water
20 ml (¾ fl oz) extra virgin olive oil
pinch of salt

Sauce

60–80 ml (¼–⅓ cup) extra virgin olive oil
2 garlic cloves, finely chopped
1 bird's eye chilli, finely sliced, or chilli flakes, to taste
800 g (1 lb 12 oz) tinned cherry tomatoes, or 500 g (1 lb 2 oz) cherry or vine-ripened tomatoes, halved
bunch of basil, leaves only, torn, plus extra to serve

To serve

grated Pecorino Romano or Parmigiano Reggiano

For the pasta

Mix, knead and rest the pasta ingredients following the instructions on pages 17–18. Place the rested dough on a work surface that has been lightly dusted with 00 flour and divide into four portions. Cover the portions so they don't dry out.

Working with one portion at a time, roll the dough into sheets using a pasta machine (see pages 18–21) or by hand (pages 21–22). Roll the pasta sheet to a thickness of 3 mm (⅛ in). Depending on your machine, this may be around setting 3.

Lightly dust the pasta sheet with fine semolina flour and fold the pasta sheet loosely a few times along the entire length of the sheet, so you have a folded tube of dough with many layers. Gently flatten the tube, then cut the dough into strips 4 mm (approx. ⅛ in) wide with a knife. Unroll the strips and place the cut strands onto a tray or a pasta drying rack that has been lightly dusted with fine semolina flour. Repeat the rolling and cutting process with the remaining dough portions and filling, then set aside until ready to cook.

For the sauce

In a large frying pan over medium heat, add the olive oil, garlic and chilli. Cook for about 3 minutes, until the garlic has softened but not browned.

Add the tomatoes and basil, and season with salt and pepper to taste. Simmer for another 20 minutes, stirring occasionally. Taste and adjust seasoning again if needed.

To cook the ciriole
Bring a large saucepan of water to the boil over high heat, then add cooking salt. Cook the ciriole for 4–5 minutes, until al dente.

Use a handled colander to transfer the cooked pasta directly into the sauce. Toss to coat well, adding a little pasta water if needed for extra creaminess.

Serve topped with grated pecorino or parmigiano.

Note
You can use dried ciriole or tagliolini instead of fresh if you prefer. You'll need about 500 g (1 lb 2 oz) for this recipe. Cook according to the packet instructions.

CIRIOLE

Ciriole is a delicacy from the province of Terni; it is a simple, rustic pasta similar to spaghetti or trenette, but with thicker strands.

Of the many ciriole recipes that I have researched, each differs in ingredients for the pasta dough. Ciriole tends to have a unique, chewy texture; it is common to use a combination of 00 flour and fine semolina flour in the dough (though some family recipes only use one flour). Similarly, some recipes include egg in the dough, but many, like mine, use a simple flour and water dough. In fact, their name comes from the Latin word 'cereus' meaning 'white like wax'.

The width of the strands can also differ across recipes, some call for the strands to be cut into thinner of about 3 mm (⅛ in), similar to trenette (page 59).

Ciriole alla Ternana

STRANGOZZI

Strangozzi is a long, rustic pasta similar to tagliatelle and pici, except that it is cut slightly thicker. The dough is traditionally eggless, made with a combination of 00 flour and fine semolina flour. Considered an ancient pasta, its exact origins are unclear, though it likely dates back to the 14th century. Its name varies from village to village — you may also see it as stringozzi, strengozzi or strongozzi.

Strangozzi con asparagi e pancetta

STRANGOZZI WITH ASPARAGUS AND PANCETTA

*
Serves 4
*

Strangozzi is typically served with black truffle or with a simple tomato sugo (sauce). I've deviated from tradition here and have called for asparagus and pancetta instead as a delicious variation from the classic pairings.

Pasta tools

pasta machine or rolling pin

Pasta

200 g (7 oz) 00 flour, plus extra for dusting
100 g (3½ oz) fine semolina flour, plus extra for dusting
150 ml (5 fl oz) water
20 ml (¾ fl oz) extra virgin olive oil
pinch of salt

Sauce

80 ml (⅓ cup) extra virgin olive oil, plus extra for drizzling
200 g (7 oz) pancetta, finely sliced into short batons
1 small onion, finely chopped
400 g (14 oz) asparagus, woody ends removed, cut into 5–6 cm (2–2½ in) pieces

To serve

grated Pecorino Romano

For the pasta

Mix, knead and rest the pasta ingredients following the instructions on pages 17–18. Place the rested dough on a work surface that has been lightly dusted with 00 flour and divide into four portions. Cover the portions so they don't dry out.

Working with one portion at a time, roll the dough into sheets using a pasta machine (see pages 18–21) or by hand (pages 21–22). Roll the pasta sheet to a thickness of 3 mm (⅛ in). Depending on your pasta machine, this may be around setting 3.

Lay the pasta sheet on the work surface with the short edge facing you. Lightly dust the pasta sheet with fine semolina flour and fold the pasta sheet loosely a few times along the entire length of the sheet, so you have a folded tube of dough with many layers. Gently flatten the tube, then cut the dough into strips 5 mm (approx. ¼ in) wide. Unroll the strips and place the cut strands onto a tray or a pasta drying rack that has been lightly dusted with fine semolina flour. Repeat the rolling and cutting process with the remaining dough portions, then set aside until ready to cook.

To cook the strangozzi and make the sauce

Heat the olive oil in a large frying pan over medium heat. Add the pancetta and cook for about 5 minutes, until nearly crispy.

Add the onion and cook for 3–4 minutes, until it softens. Add the asparagus, season with salt and pepper and cook for a further 3–5 minutes.

Meanwhile, bring a large saucepan of water to the boil over high heat, then add cooking salt. Cook the strangozzi for 4–5 minutes, or until al dente.

Use a handled colander to transfer the cooked pasta directly into the sauce. Toss well to coat, adding a little pasta water if needed for extra creaminess.

Serve drizzled with some extra olive oil and topped with grated pecorino.

‘FOUR PASTAS OF ROME’

LAZIO

Bordering the Tyrrhenian Sea, the Lazio region is perhaps best known for its capital (and the capital of Italy), Rome. This centre of ancient history and UNESCO World Heritage site draws crowds of visitors to its many ancient Roman structures, including the Colosseum, Pantheon, Roman Forum, Piazza di Spagna and numerous Baroque-style churches. Rome earned the nickname the Eternal City because the ancient Romans believed it would last forever – and today visitors can still witness landmarks that reinforce this enduring essence. There is also Vatican City, which is both a country and a city-state. This enclave within Rome is the smallest independent state in the world, and the spiritual centre of the Catholic Church.

Although it originated in Piemonte, the Slow Food movement gained momentum in Lazio following a protest in Rome in 1986, which was sparked by the opening of a fast-food chain near Piazza di Spagna. This moment helped shape the movement's mission to preserve culinary traditions and support small businesses and farmers through local initiatives.

As well as dominating the political and religious landscape of the region, Rome also takes centre stage in Lazio's cuisine. The cooking style is rustic and simple, relying on seasonal ingredients such as lamb, pork, offal, artichokes and fava beans. Well-known dishes include abbacchio (roasted lamb), carciofi alla Romana (fried artichokes) and porchetta di Ariccia (roasted pork).

Pasta dishes are central to daily life here, most famously the Four Pastas of Rome – cacio e pepe, alla gricia, alla carbonara and all'amatriciana – which feature one or more of four core ingredients: eggs, pecorino, guanciale and tomato. You'll also find simpler dishes, such as spaghetti aglio or olio e peperoncino (garlic, oil and chilli), served across the city.

FOUR PASTAS OF ROME

When you think about Rome and its everyday pasta culture, you may be imagining carbonara and cacio e pepe. These two dishes, however, are only part of a family of four Roman classics. Each uses one or more of the same four foundation ingredients — eggs, Pecorino Romano, guanciale and tomato — to create complex flavour.

Over the next few pages, we'll indulge in these four dishes of cacio e pepe, carbonara, gricia and amatriciana. They are believed to have originated with shepherds and farmers from the town of Amatrice who had used only four simple ingredients to create these bellissimo dishes.

A variety of pasta shapes can be used — spaghetti, bucatini, penne, mezze maniche and rigatoni all work well.

These dishes prove that simplicity often produces the most iconic and satisfying results — let's go!

Cacio e pepe

✶
Serves
6
✶

The name of this recipe translates simply to 'cheese and pepper' – it is a staple and the simplest of the four Roman pastas. Pecorino Romano and black pepper are emulsified to create a luscious, creamy sauce – without the need for any cream!

- 300 g (10½ oz) Pecorino Romano, grated, plus more as needed (see Note)
- 500 g (1 lb 2 oz) dried pasta of your choice (I like mezze maniche or spaghetti)
- 2 tablespoons freshly ground black pepper, plus extra to serve (optional)

Place the grated pecorino in a bowl.

Bring a large saucepan of water to the boil over high heat, then add cooking salt. Cook the pasta according to the packet instructions.

Meanwhile, heat the black pepper in a large frying pan over medium heat and toast for a few minutes, until fragrant. Keep a close eye on this and do not allow the pepper to burn as it will become bitter.

Add a ladle of starchy pasta water to the frying pan and allow it to bubble and infuse with the pepper. If it evaporates too quickly, reduce the heat and add another ladle of pasta water.

Add one ladle of starchy pasta water to the bowl of pecorino and mix well with a fork or spatula to form a paste. If it looks thin and watery, add more cheese!

When the pasta has 2 minutes of cooking time remaining, use a handled colander to transfer it directly into the frying pan with the black pepper and pasta water. Add 1–2 ladlefuls of pasta water as needed and cook for a further 2 minutes.

Turn off the heat and remove the frying pan from the stovetop.

Add the pecorino paste to the pasta, jiggling and tossing constantly until the cheese melts and incorporates into the pasta to become a thick, luscious sauce. If the sauce is still a little thick, add more pasta water.

Serve immediately with extra black pepper, if desired.

Note
It's not traditional, but a 50:50 mix of Parmigiano Reggiano and Pecorino Romano is acceptable.

Pasta alla gricia

✳
Serves
6
✳

This dish is considered the foundation of many Roman pasta dishes. It combines guanciale and Pecorino Romano and is sometimes called 'amatriciana bianca' (white amatriciana) because there are no tomatoes added to the sauce.

- 500 g (1 lb 2 oz) dried pasta (such as spaghetti, bucatini or rigatoni)
- 300 g (10½ oz) guanciale, diced
- 250 g (9 oz) Pecorino Romano, grated, as needed, plus extra to serve
- ½ teaspoon freshly ground black pepper, or to taste

Bring a large saucepan of water to the boil over high heat, then add cooking salt. Cook the pasta according to the packet instructions.

Meanwhile, heat a large frying pan over medium heat and saute the guanciale. No oil is needed as enough fat will render to coat the pasta. When the guanciale is crisp all over, remove about a third of the guanciale and reserve to use for serving.

Use a handled colander to transfer the cooked pasta directly into the frying pan and toss through the guanciale.

Add about half of the pecorino with a ladle of starchy pasta water and the pepper. Mix through to emulsify the sauce. Continue adding more pasta water and pecorino to the pan as needed, while stirring continuously to ensure a silky sauce develops.

Serve immediately, topped with extra pecorino and the reserved crispy guanciale.

Pasta alla carbonara

✳
Serves
6
✳

This dish extends the base of gricia (page 174) by including eggs to create a rich, silky sauce.

An important rule is that absolutely no cream is ever added to pasta alla carbonara – the creaminess comes only from the eggs, Pecorino Romano and a little pasta water. The only acceptable substitutions to these ingredients are pancetta instead of the guanciale and parmigiano in place of the pecorino (or you could do a 50:50 mix).

I have noted during my travels in Italy that some use all egg yolks or a combination of whole egg and egg yolks. Either way, egg yolks are vital to achieving the signature creaminess of the sauce.

500 g (1 lb 2 oz) dried pasta (I like spaghetti or mezze maniche)
6 egg yolks, whisked (or 1 egg, plus 4 egg yolks)
250 g (9 oz) Pecorino Romano, grated, plus extra to serve
250 g (9 oz) guanciale, rind removed, diced or cut into thin batons
freshly ground black pepper, to taste, plus extra to serve

Bring a large saucepan of water to the boil over high heat, then add cooking salt. Cook the pasta according to the packet instructions.

Meanwhile, whisk the egg yolks (or egg and egg yolks) in a bowl with the pecorino and season with salt and pepper. Set aside.

Heat a large frying pan over medium heat and saute the guanciale. No oil is needed as enough fat will render to coat the pasta. When the guanciale is crisp all over, remove a small portion for serving.

Use a handled colander to transfer the cooked pasta directly into the pan with the guanciale and stir through. Turn off the heat and remove the pan from the stove.

Add 100 ml (3½ fl oz) of pasta water to the egg mixture while whisking to temper the eggs, so they don't scramble. Keep a little pasta water aside in case you need to add more later.

Pour the egg mixture over the pasta and stir continuously until the sauce thickens and becomes glossy. Add black pepper to taste and, if the sauce seems too thick, add a little extra pasta water to keep it creamy and luscious.

Return the pan to low heat, while stirring continuously, for 1–2 minutes to heat through.

Serve immediately, topped with grated pecorino, black pepper and the reserved crispy guanciale.

Pasta all'amatriciana

✳
Serves
6
✳

Originating in the town of Amatrice in the late 18th century, this recipe adds tomatoes to the base of gricia (page 174). Bucatini, a spaghetti-style pasta with a hollow centre, is the traditional pairing with amatriciana, though you can choose any dried pasta of your choice.

250 g (9 oz) guanciale, rind removed, diced or cut into thin batons
400 g (14 oz) tinned whole peeled tomatoes, crushed
500 g (1 lb 2 oz) dried bucatini, or pasta of your choice
100 g (3½ oz) Pecorino Romano, grated, plus extra to serve
½ teaspoon freshly ground black pepper, plus extra to serve

Heat a large frying pan over medium heat and saute the guanciale. No oil is needed as enough fat will render to coat the pasta.

Add the tomatoes and stir through. Season to taste, then bring to a quick boil over high heat. Reduce to a simmer and cook for 15–20 minutes.

Meanwhile, bring a large saucepan of water to the boil over high heat, then add cooking salt. Cook the bucatini according to the packet instructions.

Use a handled colander to transfer the cooked bucatini directly into the sauce and toss to coat.

Remove from the heat and gradually add the pecorino, black pepper and a little starchy pasta water to loosen and create a glossy sauce, stirring thoroughly to coat.

Serve topped with grated pecorino and black pepper.

Spaghetti aglio, olio e peperoncino

SPAGHETTI WITH GARLIC, OIL AND CHILLI

✶
Serves
6
✶

This is one of my go-to recipes when our family needs a quick meal. We're taking this simple dish to the next level by adding some peperoncino (chilli), but if you're not a chilli lover, feel free to leave it out. As you're cooking, your kitchen will have a gorgeous aroma of garlic that will have your friends and family floating towards the dining table.

500 g (1 lb 2 oz) dried spaghetti
140 ml (4½ fl oz) extra virgin olive oil, or as needed
5 garlic cloves, finely chopped or crushed
2 red chillies, finely sliced or chopped
small handful of parsley, chopped, plus extra to serve
grated Pecorino Romano, to serve

Bring a large saucepan of water to the boil over high heat, then add cooking salt. Cook the spaghetti according to the packet instructions.

Meanwhile, heat the olive oil in a large frying pan over medium heat. Add the garlic and chilli and saute until the garlic is pale golden but not brown. Stir through the chopped parsley.

Add 100 ml (3½ fl oz) of pasta water to the pan to emulsify and create a silky sauce.

Use a handled colander to transfer the cooked pasta directly to the frying pan. Toss thoroughly to coat every strand of spaghetti, adding a little extra pasta water if needed for extra creaminess. Season to taste with salt and pepper and cook for a further 1 minute, stirring gently.

Serve with a drizzle of extra sauce from the pan and top with some grated pecorino and chopped parsley.

SPAGHETTI AGLIO E OLIO

This pasta dish dates back to at least the 1800s, though its origins are still debated. It was originally called 'vermicelli alla Borbonica' and favoured by King Ferdinand IV, who ruled Naples and Sicily for almost 50 years. The dish has also been linked to Campania and the Abruzzo; however, the Italian Academy of Cuisine has officially listed spaghetti aglio e olio as a typical dish of Lazio. This is a true 'less is more', cucina povera (peasant cooking) classic: simple ingredients (garlic and oil) delivering a huge hit of flavour.

Penne all'arrabbiata

SPICY-STYLE PENNE

✳
Serves 6
✳

You can decide how spicy you want to make this sauce – add a little chilli or a lot to suit how daring your tastebuds are.

500 g (1 lb 2 oz) dried penne
80 ml (⅓ cup) extra virgin olive oil, or as needed
3 garlic cloves, finely chopped or crushed
1 red chilli, finely sliced or chopped, to taste
800 g (1 lb 12 oz) tinned polpa (crushed) tomatoes
small handful of parsley, chopped
grated Pecorino Romano, to serve

Bring a large saucepan of water to the boil over high heat, then add cooking salt. Cook the penne according to the packet instructions.

Meanwhile, heat the olive oil in a large frying pan over medium heat Add the garlic and chilli and saute until the garlic is pale golden but not brown.

Add the tomatoes, stir through the parsley and simmer on medium heat for 10–15 minutes, until the sauce has thickened. Season to taste with salt and pepper.

Use a handled colander to transfer the cooked penne directly into the sauce. Toss to coat, adding a little starchy pasta water if needed to add a touch of creaminess.

Top with grated pecorino to serve.

PENNE ALL'ARRABBIATA

The word 'arrabbiata' means 'angry', which reflects the fiery nature of this spicy tomato sugo! Chilli is a staple grown in many Italian gardens, and is used readily in home kitchens, making this recipe another classic cucina povera (peasant cooking) dish, with no complicated techniques or excessive ingredient lists.

This dish doesn't date back centuries — in fact, it is believed to have originated in the 1950s. It even became renowned in two famous 1970s Italian films: *Roma* by Federico Fellini and *La Grande Bouffe* by Marco Ferreri. I love that some dishes can become movie stars too!

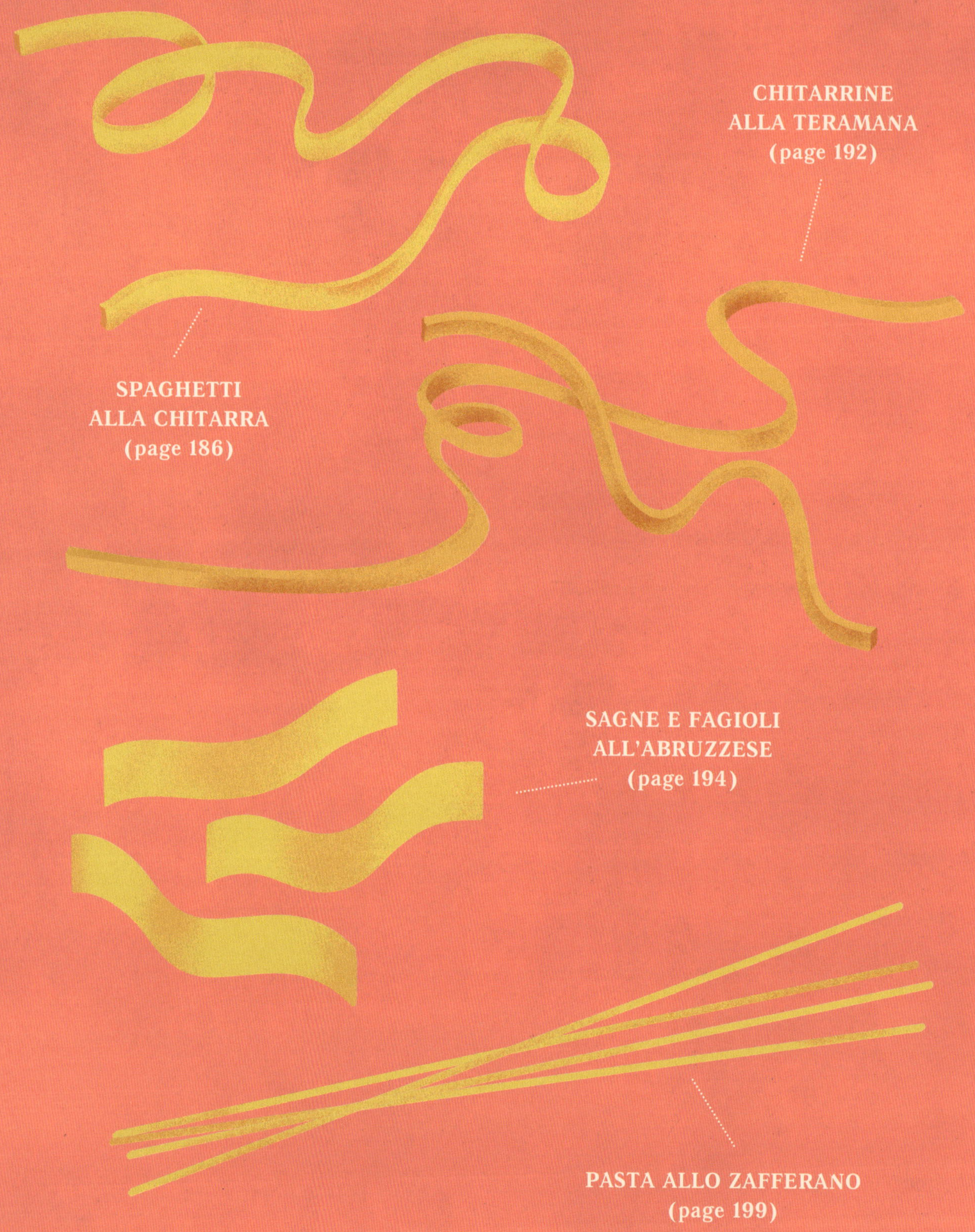
CHITARRINE ALLA TERAMANA (page 192)
SPAGHETTI ALLA CHITARRA (page 186)
SAGNE E FAGIOLI ALL'ABRUZZESE (page 194)
PASTA ALLO ZAFFERANO (page 199)

ABRUZZO

Abruzzo, located to the east of Rome and along the Adriatic coastline, is geographically in Central Italy. However, it is often described as having one foot in Central Italy and the other in Southern Italy. For the purposes of this book, I've chosen to embrace it as part of Central Italy.

Abruzzo is considered one of the greenest regions in Italy, with protected national parks such as the Parco Nazionale del Gran Sasso e Monti della Laga as well as extensive nature reserves making up a large part of the region. The region is also dotted with well-preserved medieval and Renaissance towns that have remained relatively unspoilt by mass tourism.

The capital, L'Aquila, has a blend of medieval and modern charm and is rich in architectural heritage. Visitors, however, may be more familiar with Sulmona – a picturesque city renowned for its production of confetti (sugar-coated almonds). This alone is reason enough to visit and stock up on treats to take home. Located in the Valle Peligna, Sulmona has retained its historical character and is considered a hidden gem in the heart of Abruzzo.

Abruzzese towns have, for the most part, preserved many of their local traditions, particularly when it comes to food. The cuisine is therefore often described as a relatively pure form of Italian cooking, incorporating both mountain and coastal influences. Regional specialties include arrosticini (thin lamb skewers), spaghetti alla chitarra, sagne e fagioli (pasta and beans), timballo (lasagne-style bake), brodetto alla vastese (fish soup from the comune of Vasto), parrozzo (chocolate-covered almond cake) and pizzelle (waffle-style biscuits made using farratelle irons).

These dishes are especially close to my heart and well known to my own family, as most of my relatives are from Abruzzo – from the Provincia di Pescara and its surrounds.

SPAGHETTI ALLA CHITARRA

Spaghetti alla chitarra is a traditional Abruzzese Sunday meal and is considered one of the region's signature dishes. The pasta is made from an egg dough that is cut into long strands using a wooden tool strung with wires, called a 'chitarra' (guitar). The dough is pressed through the strings with a rolling pin, producing square-edged spaghetti with a firm, rustic texture that clings onto a rich sugo (sauce) perfectly.

The first written record of the chitarra dates to 1871, when it was recorded by a notary as part of a bride's dowry. Its construction has remained largely unchanged: a beechwood frame threaded with steel strings strong enough to cut through the sfoglia (pasta sheet). Contemporary versions use stainless steel, and cheaper, plastic-string models exist — but I don't recommend them, they simply don't create the same textured result.

Spaghetti alla chitarra con sugo

SPAGHETTI ALLA CHITARRA WITH SAUCE

✳
Serves
6
✳

I've used the wider strings of my chitarra tool for this recipe. This rustic pasta takes me back to my childhood kitchen – the shape reminds me of when my mum and dad would make homemade chitarra pasta – I treasure the memories of eating this pasta with a rich, simple sugo (sauce).

Here I've chosen to share a light cherry tomato sugo, which delivers bold sweetness without a long cooking time. Adding a touch of Parmigiano Reggiano at the end is a must – it adds another level of flavour and a touch of creaminess.

Pasta tools

pasta machine
two-sided chitarra pasta cutter (see Notes)
mattarello or rolling pin

Pasta

600 g (4 cups) 00 flour, plus extra for dusting
6 eggs (about 330 g/ 11½ oz total)
pinch of salt
fine semolina flour, for dusting

Sauce

80 ml (⅓ cup) extra virgin olive oil, or as needed
2 garlic cloves, crushed
1.2 kg (2 lb 10 oz) tinned cherry tomatoes (see Notes)
small bunch of basil, plus extra leaves to serve
50 g (1¾ oz) Parmigiano Reggiano, grated, plus extra to serve

For the pasta

Mix, knead and rest the pasta ingredients (excluding the semolina flour) following the instructions on pages 17–18. Place the rested dough on a work surface that has been lightly dusted with 00 flour and divide into four portions. Cover the portions so they don't dry out.

Working with one portion at a time, roll the dough into sheets using a pasta machine (see pages 18–21) or by hand (pages 21–22). Roll the pasta sheet to a thickness of 3 mm (⅛ in). Depending on your pasta machine, this may be around setting 3.

Cut each sheet into sections about 18–20 cm (7–8 in) long and place onto a tray dusted with fine semolina flour.

Dust one side of a pasta sheet with a little more fine semolina flour, place that side down onto the wider-spaced strings of your chitarra, dust the top lightly, then run a mattarello firmly across the sheet until the spaghetti falls through the strings.

Tilt the chitarra to release the strands and place them on the prepared tray. Repeat the rolling and cutting process with the remaining dough portions, then set aside until ready to cook.

For the sauce

Warm the olive oil in a large, deep frying pan over medium heat. Add the garlic and cook until softened but not browned.

Add the cherry tomatoes, rinsing each out tin with a splash of water (this is liquid gold!) and adding it to the pan.

Add the basil, including the stalks for extra flavour, and season to taste with salt and pepper. Bring to the boil, then reduce to medium-low heat, cover and simmer for 20 minutes. Taste and adjust the seasoning, then simmer for another 10 minutes, half-covered, while you cook the pasta.

To cook the chitarra and serve

Bring a large saucepan of water to the boil over high heat, then add cooking salt. Cook the chitarra for 5 minutes, or until al dente.

Remove the basil stalks from the sauce. Use a handled colander to transfer the cooked pasta directly into the sauce. Toss to coat well, then stir through the grated parmigiano. Add a little pasta water if needed for extra creaminess.

Serve immediately, topped with extra grated parmigiano and a few basil leaves.

Notes

A chitarra can be sourced online or from homeware or kitchen supply stores that specialise in pasta tools.

Although I've used tinned cherry tomatoes in this recipe, fresh cherry tomatoes can be substituted – simply slice them in half before adding to the pan. Polpa (crushed) tomatoes can also be used; just allow an additional 10–15 minutes cooking time.

Spaghetti alla chitarra con sugo ✶ *Spaghetti alla chitarra with sauce*

CHITARRINE ALLA TERAMANA

Teramo, in the northern part of Abruzzo, is home to this iconic dish. It features the fine pasta strands of the chitarra served with miniature meatballs cooked in a tomato sugo (sauce).

It's known by several other names, including maccheroni alla chitarra e polpettine, chitarrine con le pallottine, pasta alla chitarra con pallottine alla Teramana and spaghetti alla chitarra con le pallottine. No matter the name, it's a classic example of Abruzzese comfort food — elegant, simple and deeply satisfying.

Chitarrine alla Teramana con pallottine

CHITARRINE FROM TERAMO WITH MINI MEATBALLS

✳
Serves
6
✳

We're using the same fresh chitarra pasta and sauce from my recipe on page 188, except I suggest using the side of the chitarra pasta tool with narrower-spaced wires to create a thinner pasta for this recipe.

The other difference here is the pallottine (or polpettino) – miniature meatballs to add into that luscious sugo (sauce). They can be rolled by hand, or you can use a polpettino maker for a faster option.

Pasta tools

two-sided chitarra pasta cutter (see Notes, page 189)
mattarello or rolling pin

1 × quantity Sauce (page 188)
1 × quantity Fresh chitarra (page 188)
fine semolina flour, for dusting

Pallottine

400 g (14 oz) minced (ground) beef, or a mix of beef and pork or beef and veal
1 egg (about 55 g/2 oz)
1 teaspoon salt
1 teaspoon freshly ground black pepper
50 g (1¾ oz) Parmigiano Reggiano, grated
4 tablespoons finely chopped parsley
½ teaspoon freshly grated or ground nutmeg (optional)
olive oil, for frying

To serve

grated Parmigiano Reggiano
basil leaves

Have your sauce simmering for about 40–45 minutes and prepare your chitarra pasta using the side of the chitarra tool with narrower-spaced wires to create fine pasta strands. Place the chitarrine on a lightly floured tray until ready to cook.

For the pallottine

In a large bowl, combine the minced beef, egg, salt, pepper, parmigiano, parsley and nutmeg, if using.

Line a large plate or tray with baking paper or dust lightly with flour. Dab a little oil or water onto your hands. Take a small amount of the mixture and roll between your palms to form balls that are 1–1.5 cm (½ in) in diameter. Arrange the shaped pallottine on the prepared plate or tray and set aside until ready to cook.

To cook and serve

Heat a generous amount of olive oil in a large frying pan over medium–high heat and fry the pallottine in batches until golden brown on all sides. Remove with a slotted spoon and place in a shallow bowl lined with paper towel to drain the excess oil.

Add the fried pallottine to the sauce, stir gently to coat well and simmer uncovered for 5 minutes.

You can also add the raw pallottine directly into the sauce instead of frying, if you prefer. Simply add the pallottine and simmer for a total of 15 minutes to ensure they're cooked through.

Bring a large saucepan of salted water to the boil over high heat. Add the chitarrine and cook for 3–4 minutes, until al dente. Use a handled colander to transfer the cooked pasta directly into the sauce and toss gently to coat.

Serve topped with a generous spoonful of sauce and pallottine, grated parmigiano and a few basil leaves.

SAGNE E FAGIOLI ALL'ABRUZZESE

This humble cucina povera (peasant cooking) pasta-and-bean dish resembles a thick, hearty soup and is considered a staple in Abruzzese cuisine. Although broadly called 'pasta e fagioli', in Abruzzo the traditional pasta used is sagne: short, tagliatelle-width ribbons made from an eggless dough. The pasta is cooked directly with borlotti beans in a tomato base, with some versions also including pancetta, celery and carrot to enrich the broth and deepen the flavour.

The precise origins of this dish are difficult to trace, though some theories link it to ancient Rome. One suggests that Italian sailors created the dish at sea using the few simple ingredients available to them onboard their ship; another attributes it to monks who grew the components in their monastery garden and simmered them into a nourishing meal. Whatever its beginnings, this comforting soup has been cooked in countless kitchens and brought to many tables across generations.

Sagne e fagioli all'Abruzzese

ABRUZZO-STYLE SAGNE AND BEANS

✳
Serves
4
✳

This isn't the prettiest of dishes but, in my opinion, it's the definition of comfort food! The texture sits somewhere between a thick soup and a soupy sauce, and the beauty of it is that every time I make it in my own kitchen, it's always slightly different. Sometimes I'll use more pasta or more beans; sometimes I keep the beans whole, puree them or do a mix of both. I also switch up the pasta shape and use either freshly handmade or packet pasta.

If you are using dried borlotti beans, you will need to begin this recipe the night before serving to ensure they have enough time to soak. You can make this recipe with tinned beans, see the notes for details.

Pasta tools

pasta machine or rolling pin

Pasta

300 g (2 cups) 00 flour, plus extra for dusting
1 egg (about 55 g/2 oz)
100 ml (3½ fl oz) water
pinch of salt
fine semolina flour, for dusting

Sauce

40–60 ml (1¼–2 fl oz) extra virgin olive oil
100 g (3½ oz) pancetta, finely diced (optional)
soffritto mix (1 small onion, 1 carrot and 1 celery stalk, all finely diced)
200 g (7 oz) passata (pureed tomatoes), or as needed
1 rosemary sprig
180 g (6½ oz) dried borlotti beans, soaked overnight and drained, or 400 g (14 oz) tinned borlotti beans, drained (see Notes)
500 ml (2 cups) Brodo (page 116) or water, or enough to cover the beans

For the pasta

Mix, knead and rest the pasta ingredients (excluding the semolina flour) following the instructions on pages 17–18. Place the rested dough on a work surface that has been lightly dusted with 00 flour and divide into four portions. Cover the portions so they don't dry out.

Working with one portion at a time, roll the dough into sheets using a pasta machine (see pages 18–21) or by hand (pages 21–22). Roll the pasta sheet to a thickness of 3 mm (⅛ in). Depending on your pasta machine, this may be around setting 3.

Cut each pasta sheet into long strips 4–5 cm (1½–2 in) wide, then cut across into short 0.5–1 cm (¼–⅓ in) strips. You can also cut narrow diamonds if preferred. Place the sagne onto a tray that has been lightly dusted with fine semolina flour. Repeat the rolling and cutting process with the remaining dough portions, then set aside until ready to cook.

For the sauce

In a large frying pan over medium heat, warm the olive oil. Add the pancetta, if using, and cook until lightly golden. Add the soffritto mix and saute until softened, about 8 minutes.

Add the passata and rosemary, season with salt and pepper and cook for 5–8 minutes.

Add the drained beans to the sauce, along with just enough brodo to fully cover them. Cover the pan, bring to the boil, then reduce the heat to low and simmer for about 45–60 minutes, until the beans are tender, stirring occasionally.

Remove the rosemary sprig, taste and adjust seasoning.

To serve
grated Parmigiano Reggiano (optional)
extra virgin olive oil, for drizzling (optional)

To cook the sagne
Bring a large saucepan of water to the boil over high heat, then add cooking salt. Add the sagne and cook for 3–4 minutes, or until al dente.

Use a handled colander to transfer the cooked pasta directly into the soupy bean sauce and stir to combine.

Serve immediately, topped with grated parmigiano and a drizzle of olive oil, if using.

Notes
You can use tinned beans instead of dried borlotti beans for a faster cook time. After you have added the passata and rosemary to the frying pan, add the brodo and simmer for 25–30 minutes. Then add the drained tinned beans and cook for a further 10–15 minutes, until the beans are tender. Continue as per the rest of the recipe.

If you prefer a smoother bean sauce, you can puree half the beans with a stick blender once the beans have finished cooking. Simply remove the rosemary sprig and blitz half the beans, keeping the rest whole.

Pasta allo zafferano e guanciale

PASTA WITH SAFFRON AND GUANCIALE

✳
Serves 6
✳

I adore the earthy tones of saffron and how beautifully it pairs with many ingredients. A long pasta is best in this dish, as the silky sauce coats each strand perfectly. I love using spaghetti, linguine, tagliolini or fettuccine.

- 8–12 saffron threads (see Notes)
- 200 g (7 oz) guanciale or pancetta (see Notes for vegetarian alternative)
- 50 g (1¾ oz) unsalted butter
- 20–40 ml (¾–1¼ fl oz) extra virgin olive oil
- 1 small onion, finely chopped
- 500 g (1 lb 2 oz) long dried pasta (such as spaghetti, linguine, tagliolini or fettucine)
- 50 g (1¾ oz) Pecorino Romano, grated, plus extra to serve

In a bowl, steep the saffron threads in 80–100 ml (2½–3½ fl oz) warm water and let sit for 20 minutes.

Remove the skin from the guanciale but leave a little fat attached, as it will render and add flavour to the sauce. Finely dice or cut into thin batons.

In a large frying pan over medium heat, cook the guanciale for 8–10 minutes, until lightly browned and crispy, allowing the fat to render.

Remove the crispy guanciale and its rendered fat to a bowl and set aside.

In the same pan, add the butter, olive oil and onion. Cook for 5 minutes, until the onion is softened and lightly golden. Return the crispy guanciale to the pan and combine well, keeping the rendered fat aside to use later.

Bring a large saucepan of water to the boil over high heat, then add cooking salt. Cook the pasta according to the packet instructions.

Ladle 150 ml (5 fl oz) of starchy pasta water into the frying pan with the onion and the guanciale. Add the saffron water to the pan and stir to combine. Taste and adjust seasoning with salt and pepper.

Use a handled colander to transfer the cooked pasta directly into the sauce, then pour in the reserved rendered guanciale fat. Stir continuously – the motion will help create a creamy emulsion. Add a little extra pasta water if the sauce is too dry.

Remove from the heat, add the grated pecorino and stir until creamy.

Serve topped with extra grated pecorino.

Notes

Saffron quality can vary considerably. Negin is the highest grade: long threads, deep red colour, high purity and an intense floral-earthy aroma. Sargol is mid-range and is great for cooking. Pushal is the lowest grade, with more yellow or white on the strands and a milder aroma. I tend to use sargol in my cooking.

For a vegetarian version, replace the guanciale or pancetta with a small bunch of cavolo nero (Tuscan kale), which pairs well with saffron. Rinse, chop and blanch the cavolo nero in boiling water for 2 minutes, then drain and add to the butter sauce after the onions have softened. Cook for another 2 minutes and continue as per the rest of the recipe.

PASTA ALLO ZAFFERANO

Abruzzo has a long tradition of saffron cultivation dating back to around the 14th century, when it's believed a monk brought bulbs from Spain to the region. The saffron produced here – Zafferano dell'Aquila, from the Navelli plateau in the province of L'Aquila – holds a protected designation of origin. Pasta allo zafferano is the perfect dish to celebrate this special Abruzzese crop.

Saffron pairs beautifully with sauces, seafood, risotto and pasta, and a little goes a long way. It lends a gorgeous golden colour and a subtle, earthy flavour to any dish. Because it is so labour-intensive to harvest, saffron is the world's most expensive spice and often sold in very small quantities – but even a small amount makes a simple dish feel special and chic.

MOLISE
Campobasso
PUGLIA
Bari
SARDEGNA
Napoli
CAMPANIA
Potenza
BASILICATA
Lecce
Cagliari
Cosenza
CALABRIA
Palermo
SICILIA

PART THREE

SOUTH

What comes to mind when you think of Southern Italy? Sun-drenched coastlines and beaches, delicious seafood, a relaxed pace of life, and remarkable ancient sites such as Pompeii, the Valley of the Temples and the trulli of Puglia?

The regions of the south include Campania, with its famed Amalfi Coast; Sicilia, home to extraordinary archaeological sites and Europe's largest active volcano, Mount Etna; Puglia, known for its whitewashed towns and trulli rooftops; Basilicata, famous for the ancient Sassi cave dwellings; Calabria, with its dramatic clifftop towns; and Sardegna, the largest island in the Mediterranean Sea, celebrated for its majestic coastline.

Southern Italian cuisine is defined by high-quality olive oil, an abundance of seafood – particularly anchovies and tuna – and San Marzano tomatoes, grown in volcanic soil that enhances their sweetness and subtle smoky notes. Pasta dishes here favour olive oil over cream or butter, pasta doughs are often eggless, and sauces tend to be light and seasonal, featuring seafood or simple tomato sugo (sauce) rather than heavy, hearty preparations.

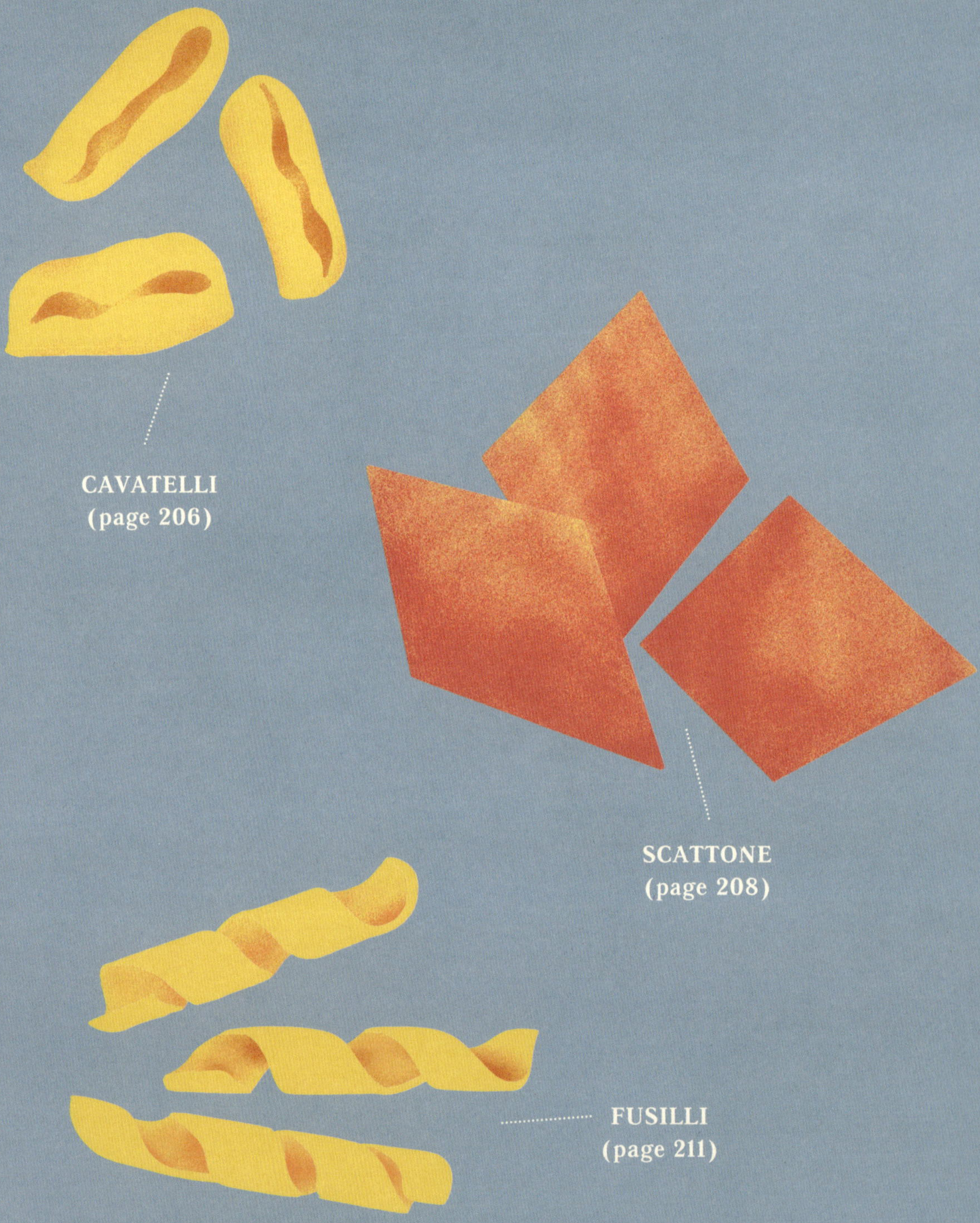
CAVATELLI
(page 206)
SCATTONE
(page 208)
FUSILLI
(page 211)

MOLISE

The capital of this mountainous region between Abruzzo and Puglia is Campobasso. Similar to its neighbouring region, Abruzzo, Molise is often seen as a transitional region between Central and Southern Italy. In fact, Abruzzo and Molise were one region until 1963, known as Abruzzi e Molise, although they have always maintained distinct identities.

Molise cuisine has a rustic cucina povera (peasant cooking) foundations and continues to embrace culinary traditions rooted in the region's strong agricultural history. The food relies on locally grown and farmed ingredients, with popular dishes including pasta served with rich lamb or goat sugo (sauce) and pampanella (a slow-cooked spicy pork dish). One particularly traditional dish is abbuoti, made from small parcels of lamb intestines filled with offal and hard-boiled eggs, then roasted with garlic, herbs and chilli. While it may not be to everyone's taste, it highlights the region's no-waste approach to cooking.

The region is also a cheese haven, with varieties such as caciocavallo, buffalo mozzarella, ricotta, pecorino and scamorza frequently appearing in pasta ripiena (filled pasta) dishes.

Molise forms part of a trio, with Lazio and Abruzzo, that is known for producing high-quality durum wheat, ideal for pasta making. Regional pasta dishes include cavatelli (often served in a ragu), fusilli in a spicy tomato sugo, and scattone — a simple dish of short pasta (typically penne, but other shapes like taccozze can be used) cooked in red wine.

Cavatelli con aglio, zucchine e pangrattato

CAVATELLI WITH GARLIC, ZUCCHINI AND TOASTED BREADCRUMBS

✶
Serves
4
✶

This recipe is simple and very quick to make. It can be made and served within 30 minutes, and the pangrattato and sauce can be prepared while the pasta dough is resting. The dough is easy to work with, requiring very little extra flour on your work surface, and the crispiness of the pangrattato – also known as 'poor man's parmesan' – is sublime and addictive, and an affordable way to add flavour and texture.

Pasta tools

garganelli or gnocchi board (optional)

Pangrattato

100 g (1¼ cups) fresh breadcrumbs
40–80 ml (1¼–2½ fl oz) extra virgin olive oil, plus extra if needed
zest of 1 lemon

Pasta

400 g (14 oz) fine semolina flour, plus extra for dusting
200 ml (7 fl oz) water
pinch of salt

Sauce

60 ml (¼ cup) extra virgin olive oil, plus extra for drizzling
80 g (2¾ oz) unsalted butter
4–5 garlic cloves, thinly sliced
3 zucchinis (courgettes), sliced into short batons (about 5–8 mm/ ¼ in thick)

For the pangrattato

In a frying pan over medium heat, add the breadcrumbs and toast until the colour changes from blonde to light brown and toasty – it darkens quickly, so don't step away from the pan!

Add half the olive oil and the lemon zest, season with salt and pepper, and stir through to infuse all the flavours. Add a little extra olive oil if the mixture seems too dry. Transfer to a large, shallow bowl to cool.

Alternatively, you can toast the breadcrumbs in the oven at 180°C (350°F) for 5–8 minutes, or until lightly browned, then stir through the remaining ingredients.

For the pasta

Mix, knead and rest the pasta ingredients following the instructions on pages 17–18. Place the rested dough on an unfloured work surface and divide into six portions. Cover the portions so they don't dry out.

Working with one portion at a time, roll the dough into a thin rope about 2 cm (¾ in) in diameter, then cut into 1 cm (½ in) pieces.

To make ridged (rigate) cavatelli, lightly dust a small, ridged garganelli or gnocchi board with fine semolina flour. Press each piece of dough with your thumb and drag it down the board so it curls and forms a hollow centre.

For smooth (lisce) cavatelli, press each piece on the work surface with your thumb and gently drag it towards you to create the same hollow centre.

Place the cavatelli onto a tray that has been lightly dusted with fine semolina flour. Repeat the rolling and shaping process with the remaining dough portions, then set aside until ready to cook. ➥

For the sauce

In a large saucepan over medium heat, warm the olive oil and the butter. Add the garlic and saute until softened but not browned. Add the zucchini and cook until the garlic and zucchini are golden. Season to taste with salt and pepper, then reduce the heat to very low until the pasta is ready.

To cook the cavatelli

Bring a large saucepan of water to the boil over high heat, then add cooking salt. Cook the pasta for 3–4 minutes, or until al dente.

Use a handled colander to transfer the cooked pasta directly into the sauce and toss to coat well, adding a little pasta water if needed for extra creaminess.

Drizzle with a little olive oil and top with pangrattato to serve.

Note

Leftover pangrattato can be stored in an airtight container for 1–2 days. Reheat briefly in a frying pan or oven to restore crispiness.

CAVATELLI

Cavatelli means 'little hollow', a nod to the small hollow centre in each piece that catches and holds on to the sauce it is served with. Made from a simple dough of fine semolina flour and water, the shape was traditionally hand-rolled on a kitchen bench to create a simple, smooth pasta, though some families used a small wooden ridged or patterned board to add texture.

This is one of the oldest known pasta shapes, with origins dating back to the 1200s, and remains popular for its ease and speed of preparation. Cavatelli can be served in many ways — with a traditional pork ragu, with seafood or with simple vegetables such as cime di rapa (rapini or broccoli rabe) in tomato sugo (sauce).

SCATTONE

Scattone originated in the rural areas of Molise, and like many cucina povera (peasant cooking) dishes, its exact beginnings are unknown — several towns claim it as their own! Traditionally served as a hot aperitivo or apericena (to open your appetite), the dish is distinctive for the addition of full-bodied red wine to the pasta water broth. The dough is made simply with fine semolina flour and water, and the pasta can take a few forms: sagne (a short, flat tagliatelle-style cut), taccozze (small diamond shapes) or even dried shapes such as mezze penne or pennette. Today, this regional specialty is celebrated with an annual scattone festival held each August in Torella del Sannio, in the province of Campobasso.

Scattone taccozze con vino rosso

SCATTONE TACCOZZE IN RED WINE

✳
Serves 8–10 small aperitivo portions
✳

My dad used to make his own wine every year, and I remember the whole process – from grape crushing through to barrel aging and bottling. A bottle of Dad's wine would always take pride of place on our dinner table, and sometimes he would add sliced peaches to a glass of red wine – pesche al vino rosso – to enhance the flavour. I know he would have loved this soupy red wine dish too!

Taccozze is my preferred pasta shape here: it's a small diamond or rhomboid form that pairs perfectly with the full-bodied red wine. Using the reserved pasta water – known as 'lavatura' in the Molise dialect – gives it extra creaminess.

Pasta tools

pasta machine or rolling pin

Pasta

300 g (10½ oz) fine semolina flour, plus extra for dusting
150 ml (5 fl oz) water
pinch of salt

Soup

750 ml (3 cups) full-bodied red wine (such as Tintilia or Montepulciano), warmed
ground red chilli, to taste (optional)

For the pasta

Mix, knead and rest the pasta ingredients following the instructions on pages 17–18. Place the rested dough on a work surface that has been lightly dusted with fine semolina flour and divide into two or three portions. Cover the portions so they don't dry out.

Working with one portion at a time, roll the dough into sheets using a pasta machine (see pages 18–21) or by hand (pages 21–22). Roll the pasta sheet to a thickness of 2 mm (approx. 1/16 in). Depending on your pasta machine, this may be between setting 5 and 6.

Cut the sheet into long strips about 2.5–4 cm (1–1½ in) wide, dust lightly with fine semolina flour, layer the strips on top of each other, then cut diagonally across at 2.5–4 cm (1–1½ in) intervals to form small diamond or rhomboid shapes. Place the scattone onto a tray that has been lightly dusted with fine semolina flour. Repeat the rolling and cutting process with the remaining dough portions, then set aside until ready to cook.

To cook the taccozze and serve

Bring a large saucepan of water to the boil over high heat, then add cooking salt. Cook the taccozze for 3–4 minutes, or until al dente.

Use a handled colander divide the pasta into individual aperitivo bowls. Ladle over 50–60 ml (¼ cup) of the pasta water into each bowl.

Add 75–100 ml (2½–3½ fl oz) red wine to each bowl, along with a pinch of pepper and chilli, if using. Serve immediately while hot. Buon aperitivo!

Fusilli alla Molisana

*
Serves
6
*

I love a bit of spice in my life, so I've chosen a spiced tomato sugo (sauce) for this dish. This flavourful sauce uses both onion and garlic, where many sugos use only one.

This spiced sugo is the perfect accompaniment for fusilli – the twirls of this pasta will catch plenty of the flavourful sugo. You can use either a wooden or a metal skewer to roll the fusilli shape.

Pasta tools

wooden or metal skewer

Pasta (see Note)

- 500 g (1 lb 2 oz) fine semolina flour, plus extra for dusting
- 250 ml (1 cup) water
- pinch of salt

Sauce

- 80 ml (⅓ cup) extra virgin olive oil
- 1 small onion, finely chopped
- 2 garlic cloves, finely chopped
- 1 bird's eye chilli, chopped, or ½ teaspoon chilli flakes
- 800 g (1 lb 12 oz) tinned polpa (crushed) tomatoes
- small bunch of basil, leaves roughly torn, plus extra leaves to serve

To serve

- grated Pecorino Romano or Parmigiano Reggiano

For the pasta

Mix, knead and rest the pasta ingredients following the instructions on pages 17–18. Place the rested dough on a work surface that has been lightly dusted with fine semolina flour and divide into four portions. Cover the portions so they don't dry out.

Working with one portion at a time, roll the dough into a thin rope about 5–8 mm (approx. ¼ in) in diameter, then cut the rope into 6 cm (2½ in) lengths. Cover the cut pieces while you shape the fusilli.

Place one piece of pasta horizontally on the work surface in front of you. Position a wooden or metal skewer on top of the dough, at a slight angle to the pasta piece. Using your palms, roll the skewer towards you so that the pasta piece curls and wraps around the skewer in a spiral. Try not to overlap the dough. Roll back and forth using medium pressure to secure a smooth shape.

Gently slide the fusilli off the skewer and place onto a tray that has been lightly dusted with fine semolina flour. Repeat the rolling, cutting and shaping process with the remaining dough portions, then set aside until ready to cook.

For the sauce

In a large frying pan over medium heat, heat the olive oil and saute the onion, garlic and chilli until the onion and garlic are softened and lightly golden but not browned.

Add the tomatoes and roughly torn basil (including the stalks, which add extra flavour and soften as they cook). Simmer for 20 minutes, until thickened. Remove the basil stalks and adjust seasoning to taste.

To cook the fusilli and serve

Bring a large saucepan of water to the boil over high heat, then add cooking salt. Cook the fusilli for 4–5 minutes, or until al dente.

Use a handled colander to transfer the cooked pasta directly into the sauce and stir to coat well.

Serve immediately, topped with grated pecorino or parmigiano and a few basil leaves. If you're daring, add more chilli!

Note

You can use dried fusilli instead of fresh if you prefer. You'll need about 500 g (1 lb 2 oz) for this recipe. Cook according to the packet instructions.

FUSILLI

Fusilli is a short pasta widely used in this region, and its corkscrew shape is believed to have Arab influences. The name comes from the Italian word 'fuso', meaning 'spindle' — which was also the name of the tool that was historically used to twist the dough into its spiral form.

Originally, the pasta was hand-rolled: a thin wooden rod was used to wrap and roll the dough to create the signature twist. Families across Italy have their own variations, from the long, elegant fusilli lunghi to the larger, chunkier fusilloni.

If hand-rolling isn't your style, dried fusilli made with a pasta extruder is easily found in supermarkets.

Fusilli alla Molisana

PASTA ALLE VONGOLE (page 216)
PASTA ALLA PUTTANESCA (page 218)
PACCHERI (page 221)

CAMPANIA

Campania is perhaps best known for the ancient ruins of Pompeii and Herculaneum, its still-active volcano, Mount Vesuvius, and its dramatic coastline – which notably includes the UNESCO World Heritage-listed Amalfi Coast.

The capital, Naples, is a lively, raw and bustling city and one of the oldest continuously inhabited urban centres in the world, dating back to the 6th century BCE. It is also the birthplace of pizza, specifically pizza Margherita, named after Queen Margherita and made using ingredients that reflect the colours of the Italian flag. Naples has also perfected street food, with much-loved offerings such as pizza fritta (fried pizza), pizza a portafoglio (folded pizza), cuoppo (a paper cone filled with mixed fried seafood or other fried items), frittatina (fried pasta), and sweet treats including zeppole, rum baba and sfogliatella.

Beyond pizza, Campania is the home of some of Italy's most iconic ingredients, including buffalo mozzarella, San Marzano tomatoes and the sweet yet potent lemon liqueur limoncello. Common regional pasta shapes include linguine, paccheri, rigatoni and ziti, alongside the celebrated dish spaghetti alle vongole.

Pasta lovers, take note: the town of Gragnano is renowned for its exceptional dried pasta and is known as the Città della Pasta (City of Pasta). In the late 1700s, local producers began making dried macaroni on a large scale, earning it the nickname 'white gold' for its nutritional value and economic importance.

Spaghetti alle vongole

SPAGHETTI WITH CLAMS

✳
Serves
6
✳

This simple and quick Neapolitan classic celebrates fresh vongole (clams) with garlic, olive oil and white wine. A long, fine pasta works best here – spaghetti and linguine both suit the delicate flavours of the vongole.

1 kg (2 lb 3 oz) vongole (clams)
500 g (1 lb 2 oz) dried spaghetti
100 ml (3½ fl oz) extra virgin olive oil
3 garlic cloves, crushed
chilli flakes, to taste
100 ml (3½ fl oz) dry white wine (such as Greco di Tufo, Fiano di Avellino or Falanghina)
small bunch of parsley, chopped
zest of 1 lemon, plus extra to serve
dried chilli flakes (optional), to serve

Start by cleaning the vongole: rinse, then place in a large bowl of cold water with a generous pinch of salt. Soak for 30–45 minutes to allow the vongole to filter and expel any sand. If a large amount of sand collects in the bowl, drain and repeat the process, allowing the vongole to soak for another 20 minutes. Drain again and soak in unsalted cold water for 10 minutes.

Bring a large saucepan of water to the boil over high heat, then add cooking salt. Cook the spaghetti according to the packet instructions.

Meanwhile, heat the oil a large frying pan over medium heat. Add the garlic, chilli flakes and a pinch of salt, then saute until the garlic has softened.

Drain the vongole well then add to the frying pan along with the white wine. Stir to coat the shells in the oil. Cook for 2 minutes to allow the wine to reduce slightly, then cover and cook for a further 3 minutes.

Use a handled colander to transfer the cooked spaghetti directly into the frying pan. Toss well and add the lemon zest, half the parsley, adding a little extra pasta water for creaminess if needed.

Remove from the heat and discard any vongole that haven't opened, and any cracked or empty shells.

Stir through the remaining parsley and serve immediately, topped with extra lemon zest and some chilli flakes, if you wish.

PASTA ALLE VONGOLE

Pasta alle vongole originated in the city of Naples around the 17th–18th century as a dish served to noble families. One early published recipe appears in *Cucina Teorico-Pratica* (1839) by Ippolito Cavalcanti, the Duke of Buonvicino. His cookbook is considered an important record and respected source of Italian culinary tradition and the history of Neapolitan cooking.

Pasta alla puttanesca

*
Serves
6
*

This classic, simple sauce (that has a slightly sultry history, see below) is made with olive oil, tomatoes, olives, capers, garlic, anchovies, parsley and peperoncino (chilli). Spaghetti is the traditional pairing with puttanesca, but fettucine, bucatini and linguine also suit this dish.

Italians have strict rules when cooking with seafood, so cheese isn't included in the recipe. I'd argue that you won't need it anyway, the saltiness of the anchovies, capers and olives offer plenty of seasoning.

- 100 ml (3½ fl oz) extra virgin olive oil
- 2 garlic cloves, finely chopped
- 1 small red chilli, finely chopped
- 5–6 anchovy fillets in oil, finely chopped
- 50 g (1¾ oz) capers, drained
- 100 g (3½ oz) black olives, pitted and halved
- 800 g (1 lb 12 oz) tinned polpa (crushed) tomatoes, or 400–500 g (14 oz–1 lb 2 oz) cherry tomatoes, deseeded and halved
- small handful of parsley, chopped
- 500 g (1 lb 2 oz) dried spaghetti

Heat the olive oil in a large frying pan over medium heat. Add the garlic, chilli and anchovies and saute until the anchovies have dissolved and the garlic has softened.

Add the capers, olives, tomatoes and half of the parsley. Stir well and simmer for 10–15 minutes. Season with salt and pepper to taste.

Meanwhile, bring a large saucepan of water to the boil over high heat, then add cooking salt. Cook the spaghetti according to the packet instructions.

Use a handled colander to transfer the cooked spaghetti directly into the sauce. Toss to coat, adding a little extra pasta water for creaminess if needed.

Stir through the remaining parsley and serve.

PASTA ALLA PUTTANESCA

This dish is a Neapolitan classic with a slightly cheeky beginning. The puttanesca story possibly began at the start of the 20th century, when the pasta was served to clients at one of the many bordellos in Naples, in the neighbourhood of Quartieri Spagnoli (Spanish Quarters). The name 'puttanesca' literally translates to 'in the style of a prostitute'.

Paccheri con zucchini, pomodoro e fior di latte

PACCHERI WITH ZUCCHINI, TOMATO AND FIOR DI LATTE

Serves 6

This paccheri dish is a real celebration of the best ingredients Campania has to offer. Campania has rich volcanic soil and produces exceptional vegetables, especially San Marzano tomatoes, cime di rapa (rapini or broccoli rabe), zucchini, artichokes – the list goes on.

I love to top this dish with torn fior di latte, a delicate fresh cow's milk cheese from the Campania and Puglia regions.

It would be so lovely to be in Campania right now, strolling to the market to buy fresh zucchini and San Marzano tomatoes. You can also use tinned San Marzano tomatoes, which makes things easier.

- 80 ml (⅓ cup) extra virgin olive oil, plus extra for drizzling
- 1 garlic clove, crushed
- 2 zucchinis (courgettes) (about 200 g/7 oz each), halved lengthwise, then sliced into semicircles
- 800 g (1 lb 12 oz) tinned whole peeled roma (plum) tomatoes (such as San Marzano), crushed, or 400–500 g (14 oz–1 lb 2 oz) fresh roma (plum) tomatoes, chopped
- small bunch of basil
- 500 g (1 lb 2 oz) dried paccheri
- 3–4 balls of fior di latte (about 200 g/7 oz total), or buffalo mozzarella or boccincini

Heat the olive oil in a large frying pan over medium heat. Add the garlic and zucchini and saute until softened and slightly browned.

Add the tomatoes and half of the basil (including the stalks – they add another level of flavour and will soften as they cook). Stir well and simmer for 15 minutes. Taste and season with salt and pepper.

Meanwhile, bring a large saucepan of water to the boil over high heat, then add cooking salt. Cook the paccheri according to the packet instructions.

Use a handled colander to lift and transfer the cooked paccheri directly into the sauce. Toss well to coat, adding a little extra pasta water for creaminess if needed. Remove the basil stalks before serving.

To serve, drizzle with a little olive oil and scatter over torn pieces of fior di latte and the remaining basil leaves.

PACCHERI

The name 'paccheri' is believed to derive from the Neapolitan word 'pacca', meaning 'slap', referring to the sound cooked paccheri makes when stirred through sauce. This pasta is a large tube shape and is typically served with robust sauces due to its size. It can also be filled and baked.

A popular legend says that during the 17th century, paccheri was used to smuggle garlic across borders where it was banned, as the large tubes were the perfect size to hide garlic cloves!

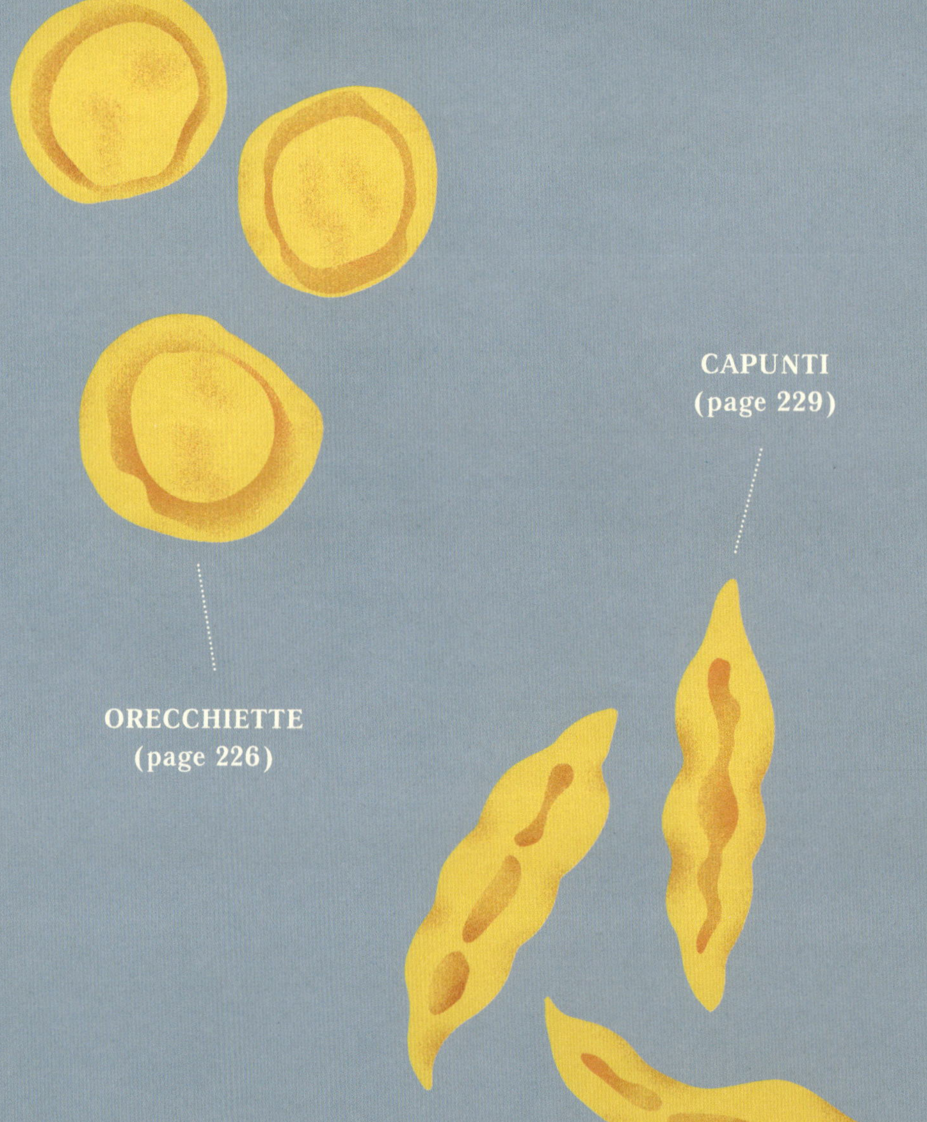
CAPUNTI
(page 229)
ORECCHIETTE
(page 226)

PUGLIA

Puglia, or Apulia, has had an interesting history, having been conquered by the Romans and later influenced by the Byzantines, Lombards and Normans, among others. History lovers can visit the beautiful trulli houses located in Alberobello and the Itria Valley. These distinctive stone homes with conical roofs date back to the 14th century and were originally built as peasant dwellings, but are now considered architectural treasures.

Known as the geographic heel of Italy, Puglia is bordered by both the Adriatic and Mediterranean Seas along the southern peninsula. Bari, the region's capital, boasts the longest waterfront promenade in Europe. Its old town, Bari Vecchia, is a maze of narrow, winding streets leading to landmarks such as the Cattedrale di San Sabino and the Fortino di Sant'Antonio. One of the city's most famous streets is Strada delle Orecchiette, where you'll often see local nonne (grandmothers) expertly hand-rolling orecchiette at a remarkably fast speed.

Puglian cuisine is generally simple and seasonal, making the most of local produce and seafood. The region is an agricultural powerhouse — it is the largest producer of olive oil and durum wheat in Italy, and also produces tomatoes, a variety of vegetables and much-loved regional specialty products such as burrata, taralli and focaccia barese.

Common pasta shapes in Puglia include capunti, cavatelli and troccoli. However, the most iconic regional dish is orecchiette alla barese, traditionally served with cime di rapa (rapini or broccoli rabe). Another popular dish is spaghetti all'assassina, which uses a deliberately unconventional cooking method: raw spaghetti is placed directly into a spicy tomato sauce and cooked without pre-boiling, breaking traditional Italian pasta rules. The result is a nearly charred, smoky and crispy texture that somehow works beautifully.

Orecchiette alla Barese

✶
Serves
4
✶

This dish is another of my favourites using cime di rapa (rapini or broccoli rabe), garlic, anchovies and chilli. I love how the orecchiette can be cooked together with cime di rapa in one pot, then stirred through the sauce. It's the perfect one-pot dish!

Pasta tools

serrated butter knife

Pasta (see Notes)

400 g (14 oz) fine semolina flour, plus extra for dusting
200 ml (7 fl oz) water
pinch of salt

Sauce

100 ml (3½ fl oz) extra virgin olive oil, plus extra for drizzling
2 garlic cloves, crushed
4 anchovy fillets in oil, drained and chopped
chilli flakes, to taste
750 g (1 lb 11 oz) cime di rapa (rapini or broccoli rabe; see Notes)

To serve

Pangrattato (page 236)
grated Pecorino Romano

For the pasta

Mix, knead and rest the pasta ingredients following the instructions on pages 17–18. Place the rested dough on a work surface that has been lightly dusted with fine semolina flour and divide into six portions. Cover the portions so they don't dry out.

Working with one portion at a time, roll the dough into a thin rope about 1–1.5 cm (½ in) in diameter.

Using a serrated butter knife, cut 1–1.5 cm (½ in) pieces from the rope and, in the same movement, press down firmly, dragging the knife towards you to create a rough texture on the surface of the pasta. Turn each piece over and use your thumb to gently invert it into the characteristic orecchiette 'little ears' shape. Place the orecchiette onto a tray that has been lightly dusted with fine semolina flour. Repeat the rolling, cutting and shaping process with the remaining dough portions, then set aside until ready to cook.

For the sauce

In a large frying pan over medium heat, add the olive oil, garlic and anchovies. Saute for 3–4 minutes, stirring, until the anchovies start to dissolve and the garlic has softened but not browned. Add the chilli flakes and stir through.

Remove from the heat until the orecchiette and cime di rapa are ready.

To cook the orecchiette and serve

Wash the cime di rapa, trim back and remove any thick leaves and coarse stalks. (These can be kept for another dish to avoid waste, see Notes.)

Keep the leaves and florets attached to the tender part of the stalks. Slice lengthways and cut into 5 cm (2 in) pieces. ➥

Bring a large saucepan of water to the boil over high heat, then add cooking salt. Add the orecchiette and cime di rapa and cook together for 4–5 minutes, until the orecchiette is al dente.

Return the frying pan containing the sauce to low heat and bring to a simmer.

Using a handled colander, transfer the cooked orecchiette and cime di rapa directly into the sauce and toss to combine well, adding a little extra pasta water for creaminess if needed.

To serve, drizzle with a little extra olive oil and sprinkle over some pangrattato and grated pecorino.

Notes

You can use store-bought orecchiette instead of making your own if you prefer. If possible, try to source fresh orecchiette, but dried can still be used. You'll need about 500 g (1 lb 2 oz) dried pasta for this recipe. Cook according to the packet instructions.

If you can't source cime di rapa, broccolini (including the stalks) is a suitable substitute.

Any offcuts from the cime di rapa can be used to make pesto, can be sauteed with garlic and olive oil to serve as a side dish, or could be added to soups or stews.

PASTA TOUR · ITALY · ITALY

ORECCHIETTE

The name 'orecchiette' means 'little ears'. This hand-shaped pasta originated in Puglia, dating back to the 12th–13th centuries, and its domed form is said to be inspired by the shape of trulli house rooftops.

Made with an eggless dough of fine durum wheat semolina flour and water, orecchiette is traditionally served with cime di rapa, but it's also delicious in a meaty ragu such as ventricina vastese, which uses salami and sausage.

Capunti con piselli e pesto di pomodoro secco cremoso

CAPUNTI WITH PEAS IN CREAMY SUN-DRIED TOMATO PESTO

✶
Serves
4
✶

Capunti is served in a variety of sauces, but I've included this recipe with a sun-dried tomato (pomodoro secchi) as it has strong links to Southern Italy, particularly the regions of Puglia and Sicilia. I love cooking with sun-dried tomatoes – they really enhance the natural sweetness of tomatoes.

I've also added some mascarpone to the pesto to balance the flavours and add a touch of creaminess. This dish is a real delight – the peas might even pop into one of the capunti 'pea-pod' indents for added cuteness!

Pasta (see Notes)
400 g (14 oz) fine semolina flour, plus extra for dusting
200 ml (7 fl oz) water
pinch of salt

Sun-dried tomato pesto
80 ml (⅓ cup) extra virgin olive oil, plus extra as needed
2 garlic cloves, peeled
200 g (7 oz) sun-dried tomatoes (see Notes)
50 g (1¾ oz) Parmigiano Reggiano or Pecorino Romano, grated, plus extra to serve
50 g (1¾ oz) toasted pine nuts or walnuts

To serve
50 ml (1¾ fl oz) extra virgin olive oil
150 g (5½ oz) frozen or fresh peas (shelled)
3–4 tablespoons mascarpone, or as desired
handful of basil leaves, to serve

For the pasta

Mix, knead and rest the pasta ingredients following the instructions on pages 17–18. Place the rested dough on a work surface that has been lightly dusted with fine semolina flour and divide into four portions. Cover the portions so they don't dry out.

Working with one portion at a time, roll the dough into a thin rope about 1 cm (½ in) in diameter, then cut the rope into 4–5 cm (1½–2 in) lengths. Roll each piece gently two or three times with slight pressure to taper the ends.

With your index, middle and ring fingertips, press into the centre of each piece and drag the dough towards you to create three indented pods. The dough will curl slightly, then flick to release. Place the capunti onto a tray that has been lightly dusted with fine semolina flour. Repeat the rolling, cutting and shaping process with the remaining dough portions, then set aside until ready to cook.

For the pesto

Meanwhile, in a mortar and pestle or food processor, combine 80 ml (⅓ cup) of the olive oil with the garlic and pound or process until the garlic is minced. Add the sun-dried tomatoes, cheese and pine nuts, and pound or process in pulses until just combined. Add more oil if needed and pound or process on a slow but continuous speed until you reach your own desired texture. Taste and adjust seasoning, adding extra cheese or oil if required. Set aside until ready to cook.

To cook the capunti and finish the sauce

In a large frying pan over medium heat, warm the olive oil, add the peas and season with salt and pepper. Cook for 4–5 minutes, until the peas have slightly softened. Remove from the heat.

Meanwhile, bring a large saucepan of water to the boil over high heat, then add cooking salt. Cook the capunti for 4–5 minutes, or until al dente.

Use a handled colander to transfer the cooked pasta directly into the frying pan and stir through the peas.

Add the mascarpone and 4–5 tablespoons of the sun-dried tomato pesto. Return the frying pan to low heat and stir to gently heat through and coat the capunti, adding a little extra pasta water for creaminess if needed.

Serve immediately, topped with grated parmigiano or pecorino and a few basil leaves.

Notes

You can use store-bought capunti instead of making your own if you prefer. If possible, try to source fresh capunti, but dried can still be used. You'll need about 500 g (1 lb 2 oz) for this recipe. Cook according to the packet instructions.

You may use sun-dried tomatoes jarred in oil or vacuum-sealed without oil. If using tomatoes in oil, drain any excess oil before adding to the pesto.

Homemade pesto can be stored in an airtight container with a thin layer of olive oil on top in the fridge for up to 5 days. Replace the oil layer each time you scoop some out – it helps the surface to not oxidise and discolour.

To freeze pesto, portion into small containers or an ice cube tray and freeze. Thaw in the fridge overnight or melt gently in a pan over low–medium heat.

CAPUNTI

Capunti takes its name from the word 'punta', meaning 'point', a reference to the two or three indentations pressed into the centre of each piece. The shape resembles a cute little open pea pod — wide through the middle with gently tapered ends — and its rugged surface holds sauces beautifully.

Made with an eggless dough of fine semolina flour and water, capunti can be served with pesto, meat, fish, hearty sauces, legumes or even in soups. A smaller version is also made and is known as 'capuntini'. How cute!

Capunti con piselli e pesto di pomodoro secco cremoso ✶ *Capunti with peas in creamy sun-dried tomato pesto*

LAGANE
(page 234)
PASTA MOLLICATA
(page 237)

BASILICATA

Basilicata neighbours the regions of Campania, Calabria and Puglia, and touches both the Tyrrhenian and Ionian Seas, though it has relatively small coastlines compared to its neighbours. The region is characterised by narrow streets and distinctive medieval architecture, found in towns such as Tursi and Acerenza.

The region of Basilicata is perhaps best known for the Sassi of Matera, a UNESCO World Heritage site of cave dwellings that are carved into the hillside, which date back thousands of years. Matera has been inhabited since the Paleolithic era and is considered one of the oldest continuously inhabited cities in the world. The Sassi cave dwellings – which include homes, churches and monasteries – are carved into the rocky mountainside and are still used today as residences, restaurants and hotels.

The cuisine of Basilicata is known as Lucanian cuisine, named after the Lucani people who inhabited the region in the 5th century BCE. It is characterised by its rural origins and reliance on simple, local ingredients. Pork and lamb are commonly used, including in Lucanian pork sausage and spezzatino di agnello (lamb stew). Seasonal produce features heavily, with ingredients such as vegetables, Rotonda DOP beans, olive oil and peppers. Popular regional cheeses include Caciocavallo Podolico and Pecorino di Filiano.

When it comes to pasta, common shapes include lagane, strascinati, rascatielli (which is similar to cavatelli), ferretti (fusilli-style) and orecchiette.

LAGANE

Lagane is a flat, wide, ribbon-style pasta that dates back to ancient Greek and Roman times. It is considered one of the oldest pasta shapes. Today it is more commonly found in the southern regions of Basilicata, Puglia and Calabria. Made with an eggless dough, it is traditionally served with ceci (chickpeas/garbanzo beans).

Lagane e ceci

LAGANE AND CHICKPEAS

✶
Serves
4
✶

Ceci remind me of my childhood – I would devour spoonfuls of them on their own. Their creamy texture suits this dish very well and pairs perfectly with the distinct flavour of rosemary. I'm sure you'll also find yourself sneaking a few spoonfuls of the ceci sauce while it simmers!

If you are using dried chickpeas you will need to begin this recipe the night before to soak them.

Pasta tools

pasta machine or rolling pin
pasta knife

Pasta

300 g (2 cups) 00 flour, plus extra for dusting
100 ml (3½ fl oz) water
pinch of salt
fine semolina flour, for dusting

Sauce

60–80 ml (¼–⅓ cup) extra virgin olive oil
2 garlic cloves, finely chopped
1 teaspoon chopped bird's eye chilli or chilli flakes
2 rosemary sprigs, leaves only
400 g (14 oz) fresh cherry tomatoes, or tinned cherry tomatoes, or passata (pureed tomatoes)
180 g (6½ oz) dried chickpeas (garbanzo beans), soaked overnight and soaking water reserved, or 400 g (14 oz) tinned chickpeas, liquid from the tin reserved

To serve

grated Parmigiano Reggiano

For the pasta

Mix, knead and rest the pasta ingredients (excluding the semolina flour) following the instructions on pages 17–18. Place the rested dough on a work surface that has been lightly dusted with 00 flour and divide into two portions. Cover the portions so they don't dry out.

Working with one portion at a time, roll the dough into sheets using a pasta machine (see pages 18–21) or by hand (pages 21–22). Roll the pasta sheet to a thickness of 2 mm (approx. 1⁄16 in). Depending on your pasta machine, this may be setting 5 or 6.

Cut the pasta sheets into long strips 2–2.5 cm (¾–1 in) wide and 10–12 cm (4–4¾ in) long. Place the lagane onto a tray that has been lightly dusted with fine semolina flour. Repeat the rolling and cutting process with the remaining dough portions, then set aside until ready to cook.

For the sauce

In a large frying pan over medium heat, warm the olive oil and add the garlic, chilli and rosemary leaves, and season with salt and pepper. Cook until softened, then add the tomatoes and simmer for 15 minutes.

Add the chickpeas along with a splash of their reserved water or the tinned chickpea liquid and cook for a further 5–10 minutes. Taste and adjust seasoning.

To cook the lagane

When the sauce is nearly ready, bring a large saucepan of water to the boil over high heat, then add cooking salt. Cook the lagane for 4–5 minutes, or until al dente.

Use a handled colander to transfer the cooked pasta directly into the sauce and stir well to coat, adding a little extra pasta water for creaminess if needed.

Serve immediately, topped with grated parmigiano.

Bucatini mollicata

BUCATINI WITH TOASTED BREADCRUMBS

✳
Serves
6
✳

This classic comes together easily and can be on the table in under 20 minutes – I think it surpasses any takeaway meal! It can be very easily be made vegetarian by replacing the anchovies with capers instead.

My pasta preference for this recipe is bucatini or mafaldine, but any long pasta works – spaghetti, tagliolini or even tagliatelle.

500 g (1 lb 2 oz) dried bucatini
80 ml (⅓ cup) extra virgin olive oil
3 garlic cloves, finely chopped
4 anchovy fillets in oil
½–1 teaspoon chilli flakes or ground chilli, to taste (optional)

Pangrattato
150 g (5½ oz) coarse breadcrumbs (see Note)
60–80 ml (¼–⅓ cup) extra virgin olive oil

To serve
small handful of parsley, chopped

For the pangrattato

In a frying pan over medium heat, add the breadcrumbs and toast until the colour changes from blonde to light brown and toasty – it darkens quickly, so don't step away from the pan!

Add half the olive oil, season with salt and pepper, and stir through to infuse all the flavours. Add a little extra olive oil if the mixture seems too dry. Transfer to a large, shallow bowl to cool.

Alternatively, you can toast the breadcrumbs in the oven at 180°C (350°F) for 5–8 minutes, or until lightly browned, then remove from the oven and stir through the olive oil.

To cook the pasta and make the sauce

Bring a large saucepan of water to the boil over high heat, then add cooking salt. Cook the bucatini according to the packet instructions.

Meanwhile, heat a large frying pan over medium heat. Add the olive oil, garlic, anchovies and chilli flakes, if using. Saute until the anchovies have dissolved into the oil and the garlic has softened but not browned. Season to taste with salt and pepper.

Use a handled colander to transfer the cooked bucatini directly into the frying pan. Toss to combine well, adding a small ladle of pasta water and continuing to stir to bring the sauce together.

Add a generous handful of the pangrattato and toss to coat the pasta. Serve topped with extra pangrattato and parsley.

Note

If you have a home like mine, where the ends of the bread loaf are always left behind, they're perfect for making breadcrumbs. Simply oven-toast them until dry, then blitz into rough crumbs in a food processor.

If you make more than you need (as I often do), store the extra breadcrumbs in an airtight container for 1–2 days. When ready to use again, just reheat briefly in the frying pan or oven to bring them back to life and make them toasty.

If using store-bought breadcrumbs, choose a kind with a rustic, coarse texture rather than fine crumbs.

PASTA MOLLICATA

The origin of this dish is difficult to pinpoint but records suggest it was first created in 976 CE in Armento, Basilicata. It is common throughout Basilicata but also in the neighbouring regions of Puglia, Calabria and Sicilia.

'Mollicata' refers to the use of breadcrumbs ('mollica' means 'crumb' or 'soft bread'). It is considered another cucina povera (peasant cooking) dish — the breadcrumbs act as a poor man's parmigiano, making use of leftover stale bread.

STRUNCATURA
(page 240)

FILEJA
(page 242)

CALABRIA

Calabria is located at the toe of the boot in south-west Italy and is surrounded by the Ionian and Tyrrhenian Seas. The capital is Catanzaro, but the main metropolis is Reggio Calabria, a coastal city that is home to the National Archaeological Museum of Magna Graecia, which houses the 2500-year-old Riace Bronzes. Greek and Italian cultural influences are strongly intertwined throughout the region.

Tropea is a charming medieval town perched on a clifftop overlooking the Tyrrhenian Sea. Visitors can swim in the spectacular turquoise waters of Tropea Beach, Marina dell'Isola, Spiaggia della Rotonda and Spiaggia dei Conigli, visit the Sanctuary of Santa Maria dell'Isola, and stroll through the centro storico (historic centre). Other popular coastal towns include Marina Grande and Palmi.

Unsurprisingly, given the region's extensive coastline, Calabrian cuisine features an abundance of seafood, including stocco (salted cod or stockfish) and pesce spada (swordfish). The food is known for its simple yet bold flavours, generous use of chilli and spices, and regional specialties such as 'nduja – a spicy, spreadable pork sausage – and Tropea's red onion, Cipolla Rossa di Tropea. Typical pasta dishes include fileja, rascatielli and sagne chine (an oven-baked dish similar to lasagna), while filled pastas are relatively uncommon in Calabria.

Struncatura con cipolle rosse, stocco e pomodoro

STRUNCATURA WITH RED ONION, SALTED COD AND TOMATO

✳
Serves 6
✳

Struncatura is usually served with 'nduja or bold, spicy sauces, but here I want to highlight ingredients from the region. Obviously, we may not be able to just hop over to Calabria to buy our red onions from Tropea, source the stocco (salted cod or stockfish) from a Calabrian fishmonger or harvest local tomatoes – but whatever you can source, the flavours of this dish will still transport you straight to Calabria.

80 ml (⅓ cup) extra virgin olive oil, plus extra as needed
2–3 cod fillets (about 450–500 g /1–1 lb 2 oz total), skins removed
500 g (1 lb 2 oz) dried struncatura or wholemeal (whole-wheat) linguine
1 red onion, halved and sliced
2 garlic cloves, finely chopped
250 g (9 oz) baby cherry tomatoes, halved
handful of parsley, chopped
chilli flakes or ground chilli (optional)

Heat the olive oil in a large frying pan over medium heat. Add the cod fillets and cook for about 2 minutes on each side, until lightly browned. Remove the pan from the heat and transfer the cod to a shallow plate and break into pieces. Set aside to cool.

Bring a large saucepan of water to the boil over high heat, then add cooking salt. Cook the struncatura according to the packet instructions.

Heat the frying pan that you used for the fish over medium heat, add a little more oil along with the onion and garlic, then saute until softened.

Add the tomatoes and saute for 4–5 minutes, until they have softened and started to collapse.

Add half of the parsley and the cooked cod pieces to the sauce. Stir to combine and season to taste with salt and pepper.

Use a handled colander to transfer the cooked pasta directly into the frying pan. Toss well to coat, adding a little pasta water if needed. Top with the remaining parsley and chilli flakes, if using. and serve immediately.

STRUNCATURA

Struncatura (or stroncatura) is a linguine-style pasta with a coarse texture and a nutty flavour. The pasta is common along the coastal towns of Gioia Tauro, Palmi and Tropea and dates back to the 18th century. This pasta was originally made from leftover wheat and bran millings swept from the floors of grain mills. In the 19th century it was deemed unhygienic and banned for human consumption.

Thankfully, modern struncatura uses a clean and consistent flour mix of wholemeal, rye and semolina, honouring its humble origins.

Fileja alla 'nduja

SPICY CALABRIAN 'NDUJA PASTA

✳
Serves
6
✳

This dish is fiery, but the flavour is rounded with a smoky heat. I have included a rough estimate for the amount of 'nduja but adjust to suit your own spicy tastebuds. Thankfully, 'nduja is now very easy to find in larger delicatessens.

- 80 ml (⅓ cup) extra virgin olive oil
- 1 garlic clove, peeled and halved
- 70–100 g (2½–3½ oz) 'nduja paste, to taste
- 400 g (14 oz) tinned polpa (crushed) tomatoes
- 500 g (1 lb 2 oz) dried fileja (see Note)
- grated Pecorino Romano, to serve

Heat a large frying pan over medium heat, then add the olive oil and garlic and cook until the garlic is lightly browned and infuses the oil. Remove the garlic clove and discard. Add the 'nduja and cook until it has melted into the oil.

Add the tomatoes, stir to combine and simmer for 20 minutes. Season to taste with salt and pepper.

Meanwhile, bring a large saucepan of water to the boil over high heat, then add cooking salt. Cook the fileja according to the packet instructions.

Use a handled colander to transfer the cooked fileja directly into the frying pan. Toss well to coat, adding a little extra pasta water for creaminess if needed.

Top with grated pecorino and serve immediately.

Note

If you aren't able to source dried fileja, use another fusilli-style pasta.

FILEJA

Fileja (pronounced 'FEE-lay-YAH') is an ancient pasta shape from the Calabrian province of Vibo Valentia, near Tropea. In the local dialect it can also be called 'filedda' or 'maccarruni'. Made with semolina (durum wheat) flour and water, the pasta is rolled around a thin wooden or metal rod called a 'danaco' (or 'dinacolo'), creating an elongated spiral shape similar to fusilli.

Fileja is traditionally served with 'nduja, a spicy, spreadable fermented pork sausage paste, or with a simple tomato and basil sauce. It can be purchased fresh or dried.

LORIGHITTAS
(page 248)
SPIZZULUS
(page 252)
MALLOREDDUS
(GNOCCHETTI SARDI)
(page 256)
CULURGIONES
(page 258)

SARDEGNA

Sardegna, or Sardinia, is an island to the west of Italy's mainland in the Mediterranean Sea. The island boasts around 2000 kilometres (1240 miles) of majestic coastline with sandy beaches, and rugged inland mountains. The earliest settlements date from the Upper Palaeolithic and Mesolithic periods through to the Bronze Age, with the Nuragic civilisation establishing Sardegna as part of a Mediterranean maritime trade network. The capital of the region is Cagliari.

The region's cuisine has been influenced by Roman, Genoese and North African cultures. Food here features an abundance of local seafood, including mussels, tuna, lobster and sea urchins, while inland dishes more commonly make use of lamb, goat and pork. Pecorino Romano is a staple cheese of the region, alongside goat's curd and the unique (and controversial) cheese casu marzu, which contains live insect larvae.

Regional pasta shapes include malloreddus, fregola, lorighittas, spizzulus and the particularly intricate filled pasta culurgiones, often described as a Sardinian dumpling.

One of the rarest pastas in the world also comes from Sardegna, from the town of Lula. Called 'su filindeu', meaning 'threads of God', it is made of incredibly fine, thread-like strands arranged into a delicate, net-like structure. Today, only a select few are invited to learn how to make this pasta through the organisation La Cucina delle Matriarche, and holding this knowledge is considered a great honour.

Lorighittas con sugo di pollo

LORIGHITTAS WITH CHICKEN SAUCE

✶
Serves
4
✶

Lorighittas is usually served with a delicious chicken sugo to celebrate All Saints' Day on 1 November. This unique, braided pasta shape is very versatile, it can be served with a wide variety of sauces, such as a tomato sugo, a seafood-based sauce or even a spicy tomato sugo with eggplant (aubergine).

Pasta
400 g (14 oz) fine semolina flour, plus extra for dusting
200 ml (7 fl oz) water
pinch of salt

Sauce
60–80 ml (¼–⅓ cup) extra virgin olive oil
1 onion, chopped
2 garlic cloves, minced
1 whole chicken (about 1.6–2 kg/3½ lb–4 lb 6 oz), jointed into 8 pieces (see Note)
100 ml (3½ fl oz) dry white wine (optional)
750 g (1 lb 11 oz) passata (pureed tomatoes)
handful of parsley, chopped, plus extra to serve
handful of basil, torn
50 g (1¾ oz) pecorino, grated, plus extra to serve

For the pasta
Mix, knead and rest the pasta ingredients following the instructions on pages 17–18. Place the rested dough on a work surface that has been lightly dusted with fine semolina flour and divide into four portions. Cover the portions so they don't dry out.

Working with one portion at a time, roll the dough into a thin rope about 2–2.5 mm (approx. 1/16– ⅛ in) in diameter, then cut into 20–25 cm (8–10 in) lengths.

Take one piece and wrap it twice around your index, middle and ring fingers, pressing the ends together to seal and create a double ring. Break off any excess dough to use when forming the next lorighitta.

Slide the loop off your fingers and intertwine the two rings on themselves to create a braided ring.

Place the lorighittas onto a tray that has been lightly dusted with fine semolina flour. Repeat the rolling and shaping process with the remaining dough portions, then set aside until ready to cook.

For the sauce
In a large, deep frying pan over low-medium heat, warm the olive oil, then add the onion and garlic. Saute for 3–4 minutes, until softened.

Add the chicken pieces and cook for about 3 minutes on each side, until they begin to turn brown. Add the white wine, if using, and cook for a further 3 minutes.

Add the passata, parsley and basil and season with salt and pepper. Cover and simmer for 40–45 minutes.

Taste and adjust seasoning if needed, then simmer uncovered for another 5 minutes.

Remove the chicken pieces and set aside to serve alongside the pasta. ➥

To cook the lorighittas

Bring a large saucepan of water to the boil over high heat, then add cooking salt. Add the lorighittas and cook for 6–7 minutes, or a few minutes longer if they are on the thicker side, until al dente.

Use a handled colander to transfer the cooked pasta directly into the sauce. Add the pecorino to the sauce and stir to coat the pasta well.

Serve topped with extra pecorino and parsley, and with the chicken on the side.

Note

If you're unfamiliar with how to 'joint' a chicken (meaning the chicken is cut into eight pieces), you can buy a whole chicken already cut, or ask your local butcher to joint it for you.

LORIGHITTAS

Lorighittas is a distinctive double-stranded and braided oval-shaped pasta made from an eggless dough of durum wheat and water. The first recorded mention dates back to the 16th century, during the period when the King of Spain ruled over Sardegna.

This intricate shape originates from the village of Morgongiori, which still celebrates it each August during a local festival, Sagra delle Lorighittas. The name comes from 'loriga', meaning 'little rings'. Once nearly extinct, lorighittas is now protected under Italy's PAT (Prodotto Agroalimentare Tradizionale) label.

Traditionally prepared for All Saints' Day, it is now made all year round. Historically, the finished shapes were laid out on round wicker trays to dry – often arranged decoratively like lace doilies.

Spizzulus con olio d'oliva, pomodorini, aglio, pecorino e basilico

SPIZZULUS IN OLIVE OIL, CHERRY TOMATO, GARLIC, PECORINO AND BASIL

✳
Serves
6
✳

These cuties are a great shape to pair with seasonal sauces. A garganelli board – which is traditionally slightly larger than a gnocchi board – is used to create their distinctive ridges.

This delicious Sardinian dish traditionally uses Pecorino Sardo, a PDO cheese made from Sardinian sheep's milk, available in dolce (mild and sweet) and maturo (salty and sharp) styles. The best part is adding a little grated Pecorino Sardo directly into the sugo (sauce), giving the sauce some creaminess and an extra sharpness. Unless you're lucky enough to be in a villa admiring views of Sardegna, where the Pecorino Sardo is easily sourced, Pecorino Romano is a perfectly suitable alternative.

Pasta tools

garganelli board
pastry scraper or butter knife

Pasta

600 g (1 lb 5 oz) fine semolina flour, plus extra for dusting
300 ml (10 fl oz) water
pinch of salt

Sauce

60–80 ml (¼–⅓ cup) extra virgin olive oil
2 garlic cloves, finely chopped
800 g (1 lb 12 oz) tinned cherry tomatoes, or 500 g (1 lb 2 oz) fresh cherry tomatoes, halved
small bunch of basil leaves
100 g (3½ oz) Pecorino Sardo or Pecorino Romano, grated

For the pasta

Mix, knead and rest the pasta ingredients following the instructions on pages 17–18. Place the rested dough on a work surface that has been lightly dusted with fine semolina flour and divide into four portions. Cover the portions so they don't dry out.

Working with one portion at a time, roll the dough into a thin rope about the thickness of a pencil, then cut the rope into 5–7 cm (2–2¾ in) lengths.

Place one piece across the garganelli board near the handle end. Using a pastry scraper, press lightly along the length of the dough piece and roll in one motion along the board to imprint ridges all the way around.

Bring the ends of the ridged piece together to form a teardrop shape and pinch firmly to seal.

Place the spizzulus onto a tray that has been lightly dusted with fine semolina flour. Repeat the rolling, cutting and shaping process with the remaining dough portions, then set aside until ready to cook. ➥

For the sauce

In a large frying pan over low-medium heat, warm the olive oil with the garlic and saute for 3–4 minutes, until the garlic has softened but not browned.

Add the tomatoes and half the basil, then simmer for 15–20 minutes. Add most of the grated pecorino and stir through, reserving a little for serving. Season to taste with salt and pepper.

To cook the spizzulus

Bring a large saucepan of water to the boil over high heat, then add cooking salt. Cook the spizzulus for 4–5 minutes, or until al dente.

Use a handled colander to transfer the cooked pasta directly into the sauce and stir to coat well, adding a little extra pasta water for creaminess if needed.

Serve immediately, topped with the remaining grated pecorino and basil leaves.

SPIZZULUS

Spizzulus originates from the small Sardinian town of Orroli. Made from a simple dough of fine semolina flour and water (or sometimes cannonau, the local red wine), this beautiful shape is formed by creating cute ridges, tiny loops and pinched ends. Its name in the local Italian dialect is 'pizzicare', meaning 'to pinch'.

The shape has remained a treasured Sardian specialty, lovingly passed down within families and often prepared for feasts and special occasions. Its ridged grooves hold sauce perfectly, whether it's a rich meat ragu or something lighter and simpler, such as olive oil with chilli and herbs.

Malloreddus alla Campidanese

✳
Serves
4
✳

This classic dish is from the province of Campidano and is served with a rich tomato sugo (sauce) made with pork sausage and saffron. I like to use pork sausages with fennel seeds, as it gives the sugo a distinct licorice-anise flavour which harmonises perfectly in this dish.

Pasta tools

malloreddus or gnocchi board (see Note)

Pasta (see Note)

400 g (14 oz) fine semolina flour, plus extra for dusting
200 ml (7 fl oz) water
pinch of salt

Sauce

9–10 saffron threads
80 ml (⅓ cup) extra virgin olive oil
400 g (14 oz) Italian pork sausage (about 1 per person), casings removed and filling crumbled into pieces
1 onion, finely chopped
2 garlic cloves, finely chopped
800 g (1 lb 12 oz) tinned polpa (crushed) tomatoes
small bunch of basil

To serve

grated pecorino

For the pasta

Mix, knead and rest the pasta ingredients following the instructions on pages 17–18. Place the rested dough on a work surface that has been lightly dusted with fine semolina flour and divide into six portions. Cover the portions so they don't dry out.

Working with one portion at a time, roll the dough into a thin rope about 1.5 cm (½ in) in diameter, then cut into 1.5 cm (½ in) lengths.

Place each piece on a malloreddus board, then press with your thumb and roll down the board so the dough curls slightly over your thumb to form a hollow centre. Lightly dust the board with fine semolina flour if the dough is sticking. Each piece should have ridges on one side and a small hollow centre.

Place the malloreddus onto a tray that has been lightly dusted with fine semolina flour. Repeat the rolling, cutting and shaping process with the remaining dough portions, then set aside until ready to cook.

For the sauce

Bloom the saffron threads in a small bowl, covering them with warm water for 10 minutes.

In a large frying pan over medium heat, add half the olive oil and the crumbled sausages. Saute until browned, then transfer to a bowl.

Add the remaining olive oil to the same pan, then saute the onion and garlic until softened. Return the browned sausage to the pan, add the tomatoes, the saffron water, and half the basil. Stir to combine and simmer for 30 minutes. ➥

To cook the malloreddus

Bring a large saucepan of water to the boil over high heat, then add cooking salt. Cook the malloreddus for 4–5 minutes, or until al dente.

Use a handled colander to transfer the cooked pasta directly into the sauce. Stir to coat well, adding a little extra pasta water for creaminess if needed.

Serve topped with grated pecorino and the remaining basil leaves.

Note

You can use store-bought dried malloreddus instead of making your own if you prefer. You'll need about 500 g (1 lb 2 oz) dried pasta for this recipe. Cook according to the packet instructions.

MALLOREDDUS (GNOCCHETTI SARDI)

Both malloreddus and gnocchetti sardi are commonly used to refer to this shape from Sardinia. Malloreddus is the authentic name (meaning little bulls or calves in Sardinian dialect), while gnocchetti sardi (little Sardinian gnocchi) is more reflective of the geographical origins of the shape. This pasta is made from an eggless dough of fine semolina flour and water, with saffron sometimes added.

Malloreddus is a centuries-old shape, traditionally made for special occasions such as festas (parties) and weddings. Its origin is linked to ancient peasant traditions of cultivating durum wheat and hand-rolling the dough against a woven round basket called a 'ciuliri', which created the distinctive ridges. Today, a malloreddus board is used — similar to the common gnocchi board but wider with deeper grooves — though either tool will work.

It resembles cavatelli from the Molise region but is slightly smaller and always shaped on a ridged board.

Malloreddus is typically served with meaty, vegetable or simple sauces such as burro e pecorino (butter and pecorino), or tomato sugo, often with sausage.

Culurgiones d'Ogliastra

✳
Serves 6–8
✳

This impressive pasta shape resembles a filled dumpling with a unique hand pleat that resembles the head of wheat. From my own experience this shape takes time to perfect, but keep persisting - it is a very rewarding pasta to create. I've filled the culurgiones with a traditional filling of potato, pecorino and mint.

Pasta tools

potato ricer
pasta machine or rolling pin
8-9 cm (3¼-3½ in) round cutter

Filling

500 g (1 lb 2 oz) all-purpose potatoes
200 g (7 oz) Pecorino Sardo, grated, plus extra to serve
20 ml (¾ fl oz) extra virgin olive oil
1 garlic clove, crushed
1 egg (about 55 g/2 oz), lightly beaten
3 tablespoons finely chopped mint
½ teaspoon freshly grated or ground nutmeg

Sauce

80 ml (⅓ cup) extra virgin olive oil, plus extra as needed
1 onion, finely chopped
750 g (1 lb 11 oz) passata (pureed tomatoes)
handful of basil leaves, plus extra for serving

Pasta

400 g (14 oz) fine semolina flour, plus extra for dusting
200 ml (7 fl oz) water
20 ml (¾ fl oz) extra virgin olive oil
pinch of salt

For the filling

Place the potatoes in a large saucepan and cover them with water. Bring to the boil over high heat and cook until easily pierced with a fork.

Drain and allow to cool for 15-20 minutes so they dry out slightly, then peel the potatoes and mash using a ricer for the finest texture. Set aside the potato to cool slightly and discard the peels.

In a large bowl, combine the potato with the remaining filling ingredients and season to taste with salt and pepper. Mix well and set aside until ready to form the culurgiones.

For the sauce

Heat the olive oil in a large frying pan over medium heat. Add the onion and saute until softened. Stir in the passata and basil, then season with salt and pepper to taste and simmer for 20-30 minutes. Simmer for a further 5-10 minutes then season to taste once more.

For the pasta

Meanwhile, mix, knead and rest the pasta ingredients following the instructions on pages 17-18. Place the rested dough on a work surface that has been lightly dusted with fine semolina flour and divide into four portions. Cover the portions so they don't dry out.

Working with one portion at a time, roll the dough into sheets using a pasta machine (see pages 18-21) or by hand (pages 21-22). Roll the pasta sheet to a thickness of 2-3 mm (1/16-⅛ in). Depending on your pasta machine, this may be between setting 5 and 9.

Cut discs in the pasta sheet using the 8-9 cm (3¼-3½ in) round cutter.

Place the filling in a piping bag (or use a tablespoon) and pipe or place a heaped tablespoon of filling in the centre of each disc.

Hold the disc in your non-dominant hand. Lift one edge to begin sealing, then use the index finger and thumb of your dominant hand to alternate pinching the left and right edges of the pasta. ➥

Continue pleating, working your way around the edge of the disc, creating a braided pattern. The first pleats of the braid will start out quite wide, but as you move closer to the end of the pasta you should finish with a narrow, pointed tip.

Make sure to braid tightly, ensuring there are no air pockets. A little excess filling may escape, but this ensures a tight braid and a firm seal.

Now, admire your nice plump culurgione creation! Place the culurgiones onto a tray that has been lightly dusted with fine semolina flour. Repeat the rolling, cutting and filling process with the remaining dough portions and filling, then set aside until ready to cook.

To cook the culurgiones

Bring a large saucepan of water to the boil over high heat, then add cooking salt. Gently place the culurgiones in the water and cook for 5–6 minutes, or until al dente.

Use a slotted spoon or handled colander to lift out the cooked pasta and either transfer the culurgiones directly into the sauce and gently stir to coat, or spoon some sauce onto each plate and arrange the culurgiones on top.

Serve immediately, topped with grated pecorino and basil leaves.

CULURGIONES

Culurgiones (pronounced 'kul-ur-jo-nes') is an ancient pasta ripiena (filled pasta) that is known by many names — including culurgionis, culurjones, culijonis, culurjonis, culurzones and angiulotus. Its distinctive hand-pinched closure forms a pattern that resembles a wheat spike, symbolising fertility, abundance and protection. The first written mention ('colurgiones con casu', meaning 'culurgiones with cheese') dates to 1811, though the tradition is undoubtedly older, having been passed down through families. Historically made for All Souls' Day and also to celebrate the wheat harvest, today this shape remains a proud emblem of the Ogliastra region.

The dough is typically made with fine semolina flour, water and lard (now often replaced with olive oil). The classic filling combines potatoes, Pecorino Sardo and mint, with some local variations adding citrus zest. Since 2015, Culurgionis d'Ogliastra has held Protected Geographical Indication status, in recognition of its protected origin and traditional preparation.

ZITI
(page 265)
PASTA ALLA
NORMA
(page 267)
PASTA CON LE SARDE
(page 268)
PASTA ALLA
CARRETTIERA
(page 271)
ANELLETTI
(page 270)

SICILIA

Sicilia, or Sicily, is the largest island in the Mediterranean Sea. It is named after the Siculi, an Italic tribe who settled the island around 1200 BCE, while earlier inhabitants included the Sicani and Elymians from approximately 3000 BCE. The Romans later conquered the island, making it the first Roman province, in the 3rd century BCE. This was preceded by periods of Phoenician and Greek settlement between the 8th and 6th centuries BCE. The Arabs and Normans also had a significant presence before the island came under Spanish rule prior to Italy's unification. This rich layering of cultures and cuisines has created Sicilia's vibrant and distinctive heritage.

Sicilia is separated from the mainland by the Strait of Messina, a distance of just 3 kilometres (1.9 miles), making it an easy train and ferry journey. Nearby is the still-active Mount Etna, the tallest active volcano in Europe, as well as the picturesque hilltop town of Taormina. Here, you can take the oldest cable car in Italy, the Funivia, which connects the historic centre with the popular beaches below.

The capital city is Palermo, though each Sicilian town has its own historic elegance and character, making it well worth exploring beyond the main cities if time allows. Several significant areas are recognised as UNESCO World Heritage Sites, including the Valley of the Temples in Agrigento, with its remarkably well preserved ancient Greek structures such as the Temple of Concordia, the Temple of Hera and the Temple of Olympian Zeus.

Sicilian cuisine reflects its diverse history and cultural influences. It features classic Mediterranean ingredients such as tomatoes, capers, citrus fruits and ricotta cheese, which is used in beloved desserts like cannoli and cassata, as well as in savoury dishes such as arancini. The island's cuisine also celebrates seafood, including swordfish, octopus, tuna, sea urchins, sardines and the prized red prawn (shrimp), gambero rosso. When it comes to pasta, you'll find shapes such as ziti, anelletti, busiate and spaccatelle, along with iconic dishes like pasta alla Norma, spaghetti alla carrettiera and pasta con le sarde (pasta with sardines).

Ziti al forno

OVEN-BAKED ZITI

✳
Serves
6
✳

Ziti pairs perfectly with a meaty ragu or a simple sugo (sauce) such as tomato or olive oil and chilli. The shorter length is commonly used in pasta al forno (baked pasta), which is how I prefer to prepare it.

Sicilian cheeses such as Pecorino Siciliano, provola or caciocavallo are perfect to use in a Sicilian ziti al forno, but mozzarella works too. I like to finish with some pecorino or even a cheesy pangrattato for an added crunch.

80 ml (⅓ cup) extra virgin olive oil, or as needed
1 garlic clove, finely chopped
750 g (1 lb 11 oz) passata (pureed tomatoes)
handful of basil leaves, plus extra to serve
500 g (1 lb 2 oz) dried short ziti
200 g (7 oz) provola cheese, shredded or diced
50 g (1¾ oz) pecorino, grated
50 g (1¾ oz) coarse dried breadcrumbs

Preheat the oven to 180°C (350°F).

Heat the olive oil in a large frying pan over medium heat. Add the garlic and saute until softened. Add the passata and basil, season with salt and pepper and simmer for 15 minutes. Taste and adjust seasoning if needed, then simmer for a further 5 minutes.

Bring a large saucepan of water to the boil over high heat, then add cooking salt. Add the ziti and cook for 2 minutes less than the packet instructions.

Use a handled colander to transfer the cooked pasta directly into the sauce. Add 200 ml (7 fl oz) of the starchy pasta water to the sauce (this will help the pasta to finish cooking in the oven) and stir to coat well.

Coat the base of a large oven dish with some of the sauce.

Start the layering process: add some of the ziti to cover the base, then scatter over some provola. Create two or three layers, finishing with the ziti on top.

In a bowl, combine the grated pecorino and breadcrumbs and sprinkle this mixture over the top layer of pasta.

Bake for 15 minutes, or until the sauce is bubbling and the topping is golden. Top with basil leaves and serve.

ZITI

A southern Italian classic, also enjoyed in nearby regions such as Campania, ziti is a tube-shaped pasta. It can be either short or long, lisce (smooth) or rigate (ridged). The name comes from the Italian word 'zita', meaning 'bride'. Traditionally served at weddings, ziti symbolises wealth and prosperity for the newlyweds.

Pasta alla Norma

✶
Serves
6
✶

You can use various pasta shapes in this dish, such as rigatoni, penne, bucatini or busiate. I've chosen rigatoni here as I think it suits this dish very well. Ricotta salata is a very common cheese in the region. It's aged and firmer than fresh ricotta, which is soft, creamy and delicate. It's the perfect cheese to garnish this dish, but if you can't source it you can use pecorino instead.

1 large eggplant (aubergine) (about 450–500 g/1–1 lb 2 oz total)
120 ml (4 fl oz) extra virgin olive oil
2 garlic cloves, crushed
800 g (1 lb 12 oz) tinned whole peeled tomatoes (crushed)
small handful of basil leaves
500 g (1 lb 2 oz) dried rigatoni
grated ricotta salata, to serve

To prepare the eggplant, slice it in half lengthways and sprinkle both sides with salt. Place the halves on a rack or in a colander to draw out excess moisture for 30 minutes, then rinse off the salt and pat dry. Cut the eggplant into 1–1.5 cm (½ in) cubes.

Heat the olive oil in a large frying pan over medium heat. Fry the eggplant until lightly golden. You may need to do this in batches to avoid the crowd from overcrowding. Turn off the heat, remove the eggplant from the pan and transfer it to a plate lined with paper towel to absorb any excess oil.

Leave some of the oil in the frying pan (you need around 80 ml/⅓ cup olive oil for the sauce, so add or remove some as necessary). Turn the heat to medium and add the garlic. Saute until the garlic has softened, then add the tomatoes. Add half the basil leaves, season with salt and pepper to taste and simmer for 15 minutes.

Simmer for a further 5 minutes. Add the fried eggplant, stir through the sauce and simmer for a further 10 minutes. Season to taste once more with salt and pepper.

Meanwhile, bring a large saucepan of water to the boil over high heat, then add cooking salt. Cook the rigatoni according to the packet instructions.

Use a handled colander to transfer the cooked rigatoni directly into the sauce. Stir to coat well, adding a little extra pasta water for creaminess if needed.

Serve immediately, topped with grated ricotta salata and the remaining basil leaves.

Note

If you prefer not to fry the eggplant, you can oven-bake it as a lighter alternative: place on a lined tray, drizzle with olive oil and bake at 180°C (350°F) for about 20–25 minutes, until golden.

PASTA ALLA NORMA

This dish originated in Catania, Sicily, in the 19th century and was previously called 'pasta con le melanzane' (pasta with eggplant/aubergine). The dish was created in honour of Catania-born Vincenzo Bellini — composer of many operas, including *Norma*. Legend has it that Italian writer and composer Nino Martoglio was so impressed with the dish that he exclaimed, 'Chista è 'na vera Norma!' (This is a true Norma!), declaring it a masterpiece.

PASTA CON LE SARDE

This ancient dish dates back to Roman and medieval cuisine and is one of Sicily's signature pastas, shaped by Arab and Mediterranean influences. It is traditionally served on St Joseph's Day in March and also on Good Friday. Pasta con le sarde is officially recognised as a Prodotto Agroalimentare Tradizionale (PAT), a designation used by the Italian government to protect regional heritage foods.

Bucatini con le sarde, finocchio e pangrattato

BUCATINI WITH SARDINES, FENNEL AND TOASTED BREADCRUMBS

✳
Serves
6
✳

This recipe is usually made with long pasta – bucatini, spaghetti or tagliolini – but ziti or penne can also be used. Because we are using seafood (and in keeping with strict Italian rules), cheese isn't included in the recipe. Instead, it's finished with crunchy pangrattato.

50 g (1¾ oz) raisins
12–14 saffron threads
1 fennel bulb with fronds, chopped, or 250–300 g/ 9–10½ oz wild fennel leaves if available
80 ml (⅓ cup) extra virgin olive oil
2 garlic cloves, crushed
1 small onion, finely chopped
3–4 anchovy fillets in oil, drained
50 g (1¾ oz) pine nuts
100 g (3½ oz) passata (pureed tomatoes)
300 g (10½ oz) fresh sardines, cleaned and roughly chopped (see Note)
500 g (1 lb 2 oz) dried bucatini

To serve

Pangrattato (page 205)
chilli flakes, to taste (optional)

Place the raisins and saffron threads in two separate small bowls. Add just enough warm water to each of the bowls to cover, then leave to allow the raisins to soften and saffron to bloom while you cook the pasta.

Bring a large saucepan of water to the boil over high heat, then add cooking salt. Add the fennel and cook for 10 minutes, or until slightly tender. Use a handled colander to lift out the fennel and set aside in a bowl. Keep the cooking water in the saucepan for the bucatini.

Heat a large frying pan over medium heat. Add the olive oil, garlic and onion and saute until softened. Add the anchovies and stir until they have dissolved into the oil.

Drain the raisins from the soaking water. Add the pine nuts, raisins and saffron water and cook for 2 minutes.

Add the passata and the cooked fennel. Simmer for 3–4 minutes.

Add the sardines and gently fold through the sauce. Season to taste with salt and pepper. Reduce the heat to low while you cook the pasta.

Bring the fennel water back to the boil and add an additional 1 teaspoon salt. Cook the bucatini according to the packet instructions.

Use a handled colander to transfer the cooked pasta directly into the sauce. Add a little of the pasta water and gently stir through.

Serve topped with pangrattato and chilli flakes, if using.

Note

You can ask your fishmonger to clean, gut and scale the sardines for you. While fresh sardines are ideal for this recipe, good-quality tinned sardines in oil are also delicious. You will need around 4–5 sardines for this recipe – simply remove them from their oil and roughly chop before cooking as per the recipe.

ANELLETTI

Anelletti is a small ring-shaped pasta, often served in brodo (broth) or sugo (sauce). One of the most iconic dishes it is used in is timballo di anelletti — a pasta bake that is made in a round tin and sliced to serve. It is also known as 'anelletti al forno' or, in Sicilian dialect, 'a pasta u furnu'.

This dish dates back to the Arab rule of Sicily from the 9th to the 11th century, a period which brought significant cultural and culinary exchange to the island. Although it originates in Palermo, it is now a beloved dish across the region, and is often baked for special family celebrations and festa (party) days or just for Sunday lunch.

Timballo di anelletti

BAKED ANELLETTI

✳
Serves
6
✳

Many families have their own baked version of timballo, but most share the same base of sugo (sauce) or ragu (with or without meat). The type of cheese can vary - pecorino, caciocavallo, provola, tuma or mozzarella are all common - but Parmigiano Reggiano works well if it's easier to find. Some versions include peas, prosciutto cotto, salami, hard-boiled eggs or eggplant (aubergine).

100 ml (3½ fl oz) extra virgin olive oil
2 garlic cloves, crushed
soffritto mix (1 onion, 1 celery stalk and 1 carrot, all finely diced)
300 g (10½ oz) minced (ground) beef
300 g (10½ oz) minced (ground) pork
100 ml (3½ fl oz) red wine (optional)
750 g (1 lb 11 oz) passata (pureed tomatoes)
handful of basil leaves
500 g (1 lb 2 oz) dried anelletti
40 g (½ cup) Pangrattato (page 236), or as needed
200 g (7 oz) caciocavallo, diced
150 g (5½ oz) prosciutto cotto, roughly chopped

Heat the olive oil in a large saucepan over medium heat. Add the garlic and soffritto mix and saute for about 10 minutes, until softened. Add the minced beef and pork and cook for a further 10–12 minutes, until browned. Add the red wine, if using, and cook until it has evaporated.

Stir in the passata and basil, season to taste with salt and pepper and leave to simmer for 30 minutes. Taste and adjust seasoning, then simmer a further 20 minutes.

Remove from the heat and allow to cool slightly.

Bring a large saucepan of water to the boil over high heat, then add cooking salt. Cook the anelletti for 3 minutes less than the packet instructions. The anelletti needs to be underdone at this stage otherwise the finished timballo will be mushy.

Use a handled colander to lift and transfer the anelletti directly into the cooled sauce, gently stirring through.

To assemble the timballo
Preheat the oven to 180°C (350°F).

Grease a deep round ovenproof dish or springform cake tin (approx. 22 cm/8¾ in in diameter) with olive oil. Sprinkle pangrattato around the base and sides to coat.

Spoon about one-third of the pasta mixture into the dish to cover the base, then scatter over half the diced caciocavallo and half the prosciutto cotto.

Add another third of the pasta mixture and repeat with the remaining caciocavallo and prosciutto cotto.

Add the final layer of pasta, press down firmly and top with a generous sprinkle of pangrattato. Press again once more to compact the layers.

Bake for 25–30 minutes, until golden.

Allow to cool for 10–15 minutes so it sets, then invert onto a serving plate and unmould. Serve warm.

MY TRIPLO RAVIOLO

Throughout my research for this book, I have discovered and been inspired by countless pasta-making traditions, legends and recipes. Some stories would bring a tear to my eye – time and time again I have witnessed the passion that so many families have for their recipes and for ensuring they are handed down to future generations. I have also witnessed the dedication that many people across Italy's regions have to protecting the regional pasta shapes and pasta recipes so that they can continue to be prepared and enjoyed authentically for decades to come.

This unique ravioli is a representation of the journey I have taken on this pasta tour of Italy. I was heavily inspired by the three large main regions we have travelled through in the pages of this book – the north, central and south. Some ingredients in this recipe are common across all three of these regions, while others are unique to one. From the pasta dough to the three distinct fillings (a nod to the Italian flag!) and the simple wine and butter sauce, each component of this recipe highlight the journey we have taken together.

I had an overwhelming rush of emotions when I created this recipe – I truly wish my parents were here to witness this. I hope you are able to enjoy this special dish with the people you love.

My triplo raviolo

✳
Serves
4
✳

This ravioli is a symbol of the Italian flag – unity, and ingredients connected across regions. I have chosen a pasta dough that reflects a blend of regional styles, while the three fillings and simple sauce highlight some of the classic ingredients that are found throughout Italy.

Pasta tools

pasta machine
3 × piping bags
patterned wooden pasta stamp (optional)

Green filling

250 g (9 oz) spinach leaves
100 g (3½ oz) cavolo nero (Tuscan kale), leaves only
40 ml (1¼ fl oz) extra virgin olive oil
125 g (4½ oz) ricotta, drained
50 g (1¾ oz) Parmigiano Reggiano, grated
1 egg (about 55 g/2 oz), lightly beaten
½ teaspoon salt
½ teaspoon freshly ground black pepper

White filling

300 g (10½ oz) ricotta, drained
50 g (1¾ oz) Parmigiano Reggiano, grated
50 g (1¾ oz) pecorino, grated
50 g (1¾ oz) Fontina or Asiago, grated
1 egg (about 55 g/2 oz), lightly beaten
½ teaspoon salt
½ teaspoon freshly ground black pepper

For the fillings

For the green filling, wash and roughly chop the spinach and cavolo nero. Heat the olive oil in a frying pan over medium heat, add the greens and saute until the leaves have just wilted. Remove and puree in a food processor until smooth. Transfer to a bowl, cool for 5 minutes, then add the remaining green-filling ingredients and mix to combine well. Transfer to a piping bag.

For the white filling, combine all white-filling ingredients in a bowl. Transfer to a second piping bag.

For the red filling, drain the sun-dried tomatoes well (this is especially important if using the type that have been packed in oil). Blitz the sun-dried tomatoes in a food processor until they form a smooth paste. Transfer the paste into a bowl, then add the remaining red-filling ingredients and combine well. Transfer to a third piping bag.

For the pasta

Mix, knead and rest the pasta ingredients following the instructions on pages 17–18. Place the rested dough on a work surface that has been lightly dusted with 00 flour and divide into four portions. Cover the portions so they don't dry out.

Working with one portion at a time, roll the dough into sheets using a pasta machine (see pages 18–21). Roll the pasta sheet to a thickness of 2 mm (approx. 1⁄16 in). Depending on your pasta machine, this may be setting 5 or 6.

To form the ravioli

Lay the pasta sheets on a lightly floured work surface. Cut rectangles measuring 11 × 9 cm (4¼ × 3½ in) for the bases and 11 × 13 cm (4¼ × 5 in) for the tops. Cover the cut pieces until ready to fill.

Red filling
150 g (5½ oz) sun-dried tomatoes
200 g (7 oz) ricotta, drained
50 g (1¾ oz) Parmigiano Reggiano, grated
40 g (1½ oz) 'nduja paste
25 g (1 oz) tomato paste (concentrated puree)
1 egg (about 55 g/2 oz), lightly beaten
½ teaspoon salt
½ teaspoon freshly ground black pepper

Pasta
400 g (14 oz) 00 flour
3 eggs, plus 3 egg yolks
20 ml (¾ fl oz) extra virgin olive oil
pinch of salt

Sauce
200 ml (7 fl oz) dry white wine
150 g (5½ oz) unsalted butter

To serve
grated Parmigiano Reggiano, freshly ground black pepper, or basil leaves

Pipe one stripe each of the green, white and red fillings onto each of the smaller rectangles of pasta to form the colours of the Italian flag, leaving a gap of 1.5 cm (½ in) between each of the fillings. Each stripe should be about 5–6 cm (2–2½ in) long.

Place one of the larger rectangles of pasta on top of each smaller rectangle and gently press around and between the fillings, using the length of a wooden skewer to press in between the fillings and help seal firmly. Press all four edges, ensuring the fillings are well enclosed and no air pockets remain.

Seal the edges using either a fork, a patterned wooden pasta stamp or another decorative method to create fancy patterned edges. Place the raviolo onto a tray that has been lightly dusted with 00 flour. Repeat the rolling, cutting and filling process with the remaining dough portions and fillings, then set aside until ready to cook.

For the sauce
In a large frying pan over medium heat, add the wine and cook for 3–4 minutes to reduce slightly. Add the butter and whisk until emulsified and creamy. Taste and season with salt to taste. Remove from the heat until ready to serve.

To cook the ravioli and serve
Bring a large saucepan of water to the boil over high heat, then add cooking salt. Add the ravioli and cook for 4–5 minutes, or until al dente.

Towards the end of cooking, return the sauce to medium heat and whisk a small ladleful of pasta water into the sauce. Cook for 1–2 minutes. Continue to whisk, ensuring the wine and butter have emulsified to a smooth and creamy sauce.

Use a handled colander to transfer the cooked ravioli directly into the sauce and gently coat in the sauce, adding a little extra pasta water for creaminess if needed.

Serve one raviolo per plate, spoon over some more of the luscious butter-wine sauce and finish with grated parmigiano, black pepper or basil leaves.

My triplo raviolo

GRAZIE

Researching the many regional pasta shapes of Italy has been a long and rewarding road. It is obvious to me that as Italians, we all truly hold onto our traditions, ensuring the past will never be forgotten and that it will be shared with present and future generations.

To my husband, thank you for your patience, for being my in-house recipe taster and for braving my weird and quirky recipe ideas. Thank you for walking this journey with me and for being part of this cookbook by sharing your own family traditions too. To my two beautiful children, thank you for putting up with my pasta creations. I know at times you reached your limit to the amount of pasta I would serve, but I am so happy you witnessed this process with me.

My nonni (grandparents), sadly were not part of my life growing up but I never tire of hearing every story about their lives – I crave and always want to know more. Even though you are not here, I still feel your presence in our shared memories and in the Abruzzese recipes that have been handed down to me from my beautiful mum.

To my parents, thank you! You are now no longer here with us but you would be so proud of how tightly we are holding on to all you've taught us. When creating pasta, I will always remember mum's strict instructions: 'patience', 'feel the dough', 'taste' and, most importantly, 'enjoy'. I still fondly remember memories of walking through dad's vegetable garden with him, watching all the seasonal deliciousness growing, which would eventually make its way onto our table.

To my sister, my nephew and his little family, thank you! You know how crazy I am when it comes to food and you still love me anyway. Thank you for being my taste testers and continuing this journey also. To my cousins and the rest of my family, thank you! Let's continue our stories and never forget.

To my many beautiful friends, thank you! Your support and friendship means so much to me. I adore our combined passion for pasta, being foodies, travel, coffee, dolci and laughter. You all know I'll always make you eat more pasta and cake!

Thank you to Costante Imports, my pasta tool legends – you are friends that are like family. Thank you to That's Amore Cheese, my cheese legends, who supplied a colossal amount of cheese for this book. Thank you to my friends at Pane e Pizzico-Molino Pasini-NextGen Foods & PEP Baking for supplying amazing, high-quality flour for the book.

To the many chefs and foodies that have become friends over the years, thank you! The generosity many of you have shown by sharing your experience and enthusiasm with me is inspirational.

To the whole Smith Street Books team, thank you for believing my idea had a place in the cookbook world, and for agreeing that everyone needed to be nourished with many plates of pasta!

Thank you to my publisher, Megan Cuthbert, and editor, Elena Callcott, your patience, guidance, final edits at the eleventh hour and encouragement to keep going will never be forgotten.

Thank you to the legends from my photoshoot, photographer Rochelle Eagle, stylist Lee Blaylock and Elise Pulbrook and Scott Bagnell who helped me in the kitchen. I adored the days we spent together, creating all 66 pasta dishes. Together we cooked, tasted, filled our fridges with pasta for days and danced through the kitchen with laughter. To the gifted editorial, design and production team, consisting of copyeditor Ana Jacobsen, designer and illustrator Emily O'Neill, proofreader Penny Mansley and indexer Max McMaster. This whole team transformed my pasta book into a stunning and beautiful cookbook.

Thank you!

INDEX

D

E

F

G

I

K

L

M

N

O

P

R

S

T

U

V

W

Z